PLAYING
TO
WIN

JERRY JONES
AND THE
DALLAS COWBOYS

David Magee

TRIUMPH BOOKS

Library of Congress Cataloging-in-Publication Data
Magee, David, 1965–
    Playing to win : Jerry Jones and the Dallas Cowboys / David Magee.
        p. cm.
    Includes bibliographical references.
    ISBN-13: 978-1-60078-124-7
    ISBN-10: 1-60078-124-1
        1. Jones, Jerry, 1942– 2. Football team owners—Biography—Texas. 3. Dallas Cowboys (Football team) I. Title.
        GV939.J64M34 2008
        796.332092—dc22
    [B]
                                                                    2008006607

This book is available in quantity at special discounts for your group or organization. For further information, contact:
    Triumph Books
    542 South Dearborn Street
    Suite 750
    Chicago, Illinois 60605
    (312) 939-3330
    Fax (312) 663-3557

Printed in U.S.A.
ISBN: 978-1-60078-124-7
Design by Sue Knopf
Photos courtesy of the Dallas Cowboys unless otherwise indicated.

For my mother

Contents

Preface

"No longer is he [Jones] the butt of jokes. He now is a part of NFL royalty. It has been a circuitous journey."

–Columnist Jean-Jacques Taylor,
The Dallas Morning News

Preface

When I began this book, the Dallas Cowboys had not won a playoff game in more than a decade and the upcoming season presented a slew of question marks. Perhaps chief among them was the addition of a new head coach—Wade Phillips, who had a less-than-spectacular postseason record in previous stops as a lead field general. Phillips was replacing Bill Parcells, who in previous coaching stints had all the right answers, but quit in Dallas after four seasons because of mounting frustration and just two unsuccessful postseason appearances.

I was not in search of the most winning team of the moment for my story, though. Determining how the once-mediocre NFL became a model for professional sports leagues in just two decades would have taken me elsewhere had recent playoff success been the only criteria. It would have led me to Indianapolis, where the Colts were fresh from a victory in Super Bowl XLI, or to New England, where despite losing to the Giants in Super Bowl XLII, the Patriots remained entrenched as one of the NFL's superpowers on the playing field. But in early 2007, when the Dallas Cowboys franchise was just months removed from an unfathomable 21–20 Wild Card playoff game loss at Seattle, ending another season in frustration, I arrived in the heart of Texas to explore the NFL's ascension as the world's preeminent professional sports league.

The Seattle loss was memorable, if not recurrently nightmarish for the Cowboys and their fans. The game-defining play was shown so many times on sports networks and news shows after the game, who could forget? Budding star quarterback Tony Romo was holding on the snap for an apparent game-winning, chip-shot field goal late in the fourth quarter with the Cowboys trailing 21–20. Finally, the postseason drought would end. But Romo bobbled the ball, forcing the kicker to abort the attempt. Romo picked up the ball and scrambled, lunging for the goal in desperation as the Seahawks defense closed in, making the stop and leaving the Cowboys two yards short of victory in heartbreaking defeat. Romo was inconsolable in the locker room after the game. The loss was the type that has the power to turn the most optimistic and competitive people into nerve-rattled doubters, destroying careers of coaches and players in a single blow. For Parcells, the loss was simply too much, a final weight stacked on several years of mounting frustration. For Romo, a question mark hung heavily over his head during the off-season.

So on the surface, questioning the locale for this project was fair in the spring of 2007, since Dallas was not the same football powerhouse it had been in the 1990s. That was the memorable period when the Cowboys earned Team of the Decade distinction as owner and general manager Jerry Jones led a colorful cast of coaches and players, including Jimmy Johnson, Barry Switzer, Michael Irvin, Emmitt Smith, Troy Aikman, and dozens of others to three Super Bowl victories and seemingly endless attention in the professional sports world. But even though the years following Dallas's historic run had not resulted in similar on-field prowess, it quickly became obvious as I began nosing around Dallas that I was in precisely the right spot to better understand how the game of American professional football had so drastically changed in two decades.

Anyone familiar with trends in the parity-plagued, hypercompetitive NFL could see Dallas was poised to return to its winning ways. The franchise had won big before and would undoubtedly rise to greatness again; probably sooner rather than later considering a talented cast of players and coaches was assembled. What drew me to the story, however, was not gridiron promise but the discovery of a burning, insatiable desire to be the best that was present throughout the organization. This was more than a simple hunger to come out on top, more than lip service supporting the obligatorily verbalized search for excellence; the prevailing culture I found in Dallas was one of fierce competitive neces-sity. I have not yet met the person who does not want to win, of course. But neither have I met the person who works harder every breathing minute to gain an edge than team owner and general manager Jerry Jones, who creates the spirit and preoccupation with winning that so predominantly pervades the Dallas Cowboys franchise.

Here was Jones, ranked by all accounts among the world's rich-est individuals, able to take leisurely days in the off-season away from the job and do anything but worry over something like the outcome of football games. Already possessing at the time not one, not two, but three Super Bowl championship rings as team owner and general manager, he could be content, basking in the previous season's regular-season record and the unequaled profits and popularity of both the Cowboys franchise and the NFL as a whole. Instead, Jones was work-ing harder than ever before in his career spanning almost 20 years as owner and general manager of the team. He was bolstering the team's offensive line through off-season acquisitions, personally hiring new coaches, and investing across the board in anything that might help the Cowboys earn another Super Bowl ring.

At the same time, Jones was building a stadium—and not just any stadium. The new $1.2 billion Cowboys home under construction in Arlington, Texas, promising to inspire awe in the most hardened observers, was being overseen by Jones the way a homeowner manages a custom design, making such detailed and specific decisions as floor-ing and wall finish selections and driving multiple times each week to the construction site. In his spare time, Jones and the Cowboys were putting finishing touches on a bid to host Dallas's first-ever Super Bowl (2011)—at the Cowboys' new stadium, of course—and planning to unveil in San Antonio the most ambitious, fan-friendly training camp ever attempted by a football team. If it all sounds like a lot, these are just routine days in the off-season for the owner, manager, and fran-chise that finds no satisfaction in being anything but the very best.

Looking back over the years that Jones has owned and operated the Dallas Cowboys, such frenetic activity and concentration on victory both on and off the field have been the norm. Some franchises may have won more lately, but few if any have had a more dramatic overall impact on the game and the NFL than the Cowboys in a two-decade period of dramatic change. Consider only that when Jones purchased the Dallas Cowboys, more than half the NFL's teams were losing money. Attendance figures at aging stadiums dotting America's landscape were sagging. The television network that long controlled lead league broadcast rights was actually negotiating with the league to pay *less* money in the future for the right to show weekly games. Network executives argued its NFL contract was just not conducive to operating profitably.

Nearly two decades later, though, the league is a powerhouse of sport and enterprise that easily trumps its professional peers in terms of popularity, proliferation, and profitability. Baseball purists might disagree, suggesting that America's game is played on a diamond, but facts show otherwise. Consider that eight of the 15 most-watched television programs of all time are NFL Super Bowls; that twice as many respondents to a 2007 poll listed professional football as their favorite over baseball, whereas two decades before a similar poll showed the sports as equals; that the average NFL fan now earns more than $10,000 per year more than the average Major League Baseball fan, providing irresistible opportunity for advertisers; and that revenues and profitability per team in the league have increased more than fivefold since 1990.

The most natural course of study to determine how all this happened might have been to investigate the league as a whole as opposed to one individual team, but it seemed to me the more telling and revealing approach might come from specifics, as in the one team and the one owner and one general manager involved in many of the most impacting aspects. That is why when I sought direction for this angle, roads led not to Indianapolis or New York or New England but directly into the heart of Texas, residence of Jerry Jones and the Dallas Cowboys. I followed the path, taking the first trip in investigation without really knowing what to expect.

What I found was a fierce competitor the likes of which I have not encountered before. Over nine months of all-access research—including dozens of interviews, one-on-one sessions with Jones himself, visits to the Cowboys locker room, and strolls along sidelines in some of the biggest games during a captivating season filled with circumstance, celebration, and even more heartbreak—I discovered a man, and, therefore, a franchise, consumed with being the best, period. Some seasons, it has worked out that way for Jerry Jones and the Dallas Cowboys. Jones, after all, led the Cowboys to three Super Bowl wins in four years in the 1990s, made a beleaguered franchise the most valuable sports entity in the world, and is building a new billion-dollar stadium that promises to be one of the most dramatic and interactive spectator sports facilities ever built. Jones also helped, according to some fellow NFL team owners, change the fortunes of the entire league by exposing new sources of revenue and actively building on existing strengths.

Few, if any, owners in professional sports have been as visible and arguably effective as Jones. The same can be said for Jones among his peers of team general managers: in a 2007 survey, *Forbes* magazine ranked Jones one of the best in professional sports, ahead of contemporaries like baseball's Billy Beane (general manager, Oakland A's) and Scott Pioli of the New England Patriots.

But life as Jerry Jones is not always easy. Mistakes and losing seasons are part of his roller-coaster career as well. A self-described lightning rod for controversy, Jones is actively involved in how the game is played both on and off the field with a hands-on approach that remains nontraditional almost two decades after he burst onto the scene. This style often places the man, and, consequently, the team, in the center of controversy, resulting in a persona that causes nearly all fans in the sporting world to have the strongest of feelings. Some love Jerry Jones and the Dallas Cowboys; others just love to see them both lose. But no one looking closely will deny their competitive fire and desire to be the best in one of the world's most competitive games.

This is their story.

Acknowledgments

A writer is nothing without a good agent. Publishing has lots of deal-makers, but I am fortunate to have one who not only gets the project sold but also shapes it from start to finish with the most discerning, reaching eye. That is why I would be remiss not to thank Esmond Harmsworth of Zachary Schuster Harmsworth Literary first and foremost for this book. When I first told him of my idea, he was enthusiastic. Yet he waited patiently, contributing sound advice over several months before selling it so that we could give a big story its best chance for success.

At Triumph Books, a special thanks to Tom Bast, who loved this story from the moment he heard about it. The entire team at America's best sports publishing imprint was committed from the start and sought to expose every angle that would help make it a marketplace winner. An author can ask for nothing more. Also thanks to Triumph's developmental editor Adam Motin who shepherded the title through production from submission to publication.

Many members of the Dallas Cowboys organization played vital roles, particularly director of public relations Rich Dalrymple. During long months of research, which began in the spring of one year and ended in the winter of another, I was appreciative that all doors were open and both my demands and persistence were always met with graciousness and openness, allowing the story to properly unfold.

Among others who deserve mention is Kent Magee. She suggests on a regular basis, wisely, that the biggest stories are the only ones worth tackling. For that and much more, I am appreciative. I must also mention Miller and Karen Welborn, good friends who loaned the perfect writing spot at just the right moment. One may not see the high country of western North Carolina as a place to be in the cold, final days of January, but with a warm fire burning, sleet pellets falling, and mountain peaks calling, I was able to finish this book in a quiet setting any writer would crave. To my friends, thank you for use of your Cashier's home and the accompanying wintertime tranquility found 3,500 feet above sea level.

America's Team Struggles

"If this doesn't work, I'd be known as the idiot who wanted to coach so bad he blew it all. So this has to work."

—*Jerry Jones*

1

America's Team Struggles

Jerry Jones did not buy the Dallas Cowboys to make money. He couldn't have. The franchise was broke when former team owner H.R. "Bum" Bright put the team on the market in early 1989. You would not have known it by walking around the team's posh Irving, Texas, Cowboys Center offices. Shaped like a miniature, sports-appointed Pentagon, the Cowboys' new administrative offices were unequaled in the National Football League, a testament to leftover mentality from the go-go oil and real estate days that fueled robust commerce in the North Texas city in the 1970s and early 1980s. Everything looked good, on the shiny surface. Legendary head coach Tom Landry was still earning his paycheck when the team was for sale in 1989. So was longtime president and general manager Tex Schramm.

Visitors to the Cowboys headquarters could walk down hallways of the finely appointed facility, passing photos of some of the greatest teams to have ever played professional football. That was Landry, who coached Dallas for one year shy of three decades, taking the team to five Super Bowl appearances, posing in one photo after another. On the job since 1960, Landry became the Cowboys' first and only coach for almost 30 years at the urging of longtime New York Giants owner Wellington Mara. An assistant coach for the Giants during some of the franchise's best years in the 1950s, Landry earned a profound respect from Mara, whom he viewed as a highly respected friend and mentor. When Schramm went looking for a coach for Dallas's expansion franchise, it was Mara who suggested Landry might be the man for the job.

History, of course, proved the recommendation was a good one. Visitors to the Cowboys offices need only to see the photos lining the walls framing history for evidence. Take the 1977 Cowboys team photo as one example. Fronted by a Super Bowl–winning roster including future Pro Football Hall of Famers Roger Staubach and Randy White, Landry stands tall as the obvious leader of America's Team. The distinctive moniker was given to the Dallas franchise in the late 1970s after the Cowboys lost to the Steelers in Super Bowl XIII. NFL Films coined the phrase "America's Team," because it needed a memorable name to anchor either side of the "versus" in the title page, as in, World Champions versus America's Team. Landry, a quiet, typically stoic traditionalist, did not take to the name at first, but eventually it stuck anyway and he and the franchise came to accept and embrace the adulation.

The moniker and the posh headquarters and the tradition diminished on the surface the harsh reality facing the Cowboys at the end of the 1988 season. Even Schramm, the quintessential sports marketer who first taught the NFL that it could be more than one set of helmets playing against another on Sunday afternoons, was undeterred by the reality facing the 30-year-old football franchise. Schramm became one of the most powerful GMs in the history of professional sports because team owners—including Clint Murchison Jr., an oilman who purchased the expansion franchise for $600,000 in 1959, and Bum Bright, the team's second owner who eventually sold the Cowboys to Jerry Jones— yielded to him on everything from draft picks to league meetings.

Schramm, who died in 2003 shortly after learning he would be inducted into the Cowboys' Ring of Honor, got his football executive start with the Los Angeles Rams in the 1950s before moving to his beloved state of Texas to run the Cowboys. As general manager, he knew everything one could possibly know about the franchise, more even than the team owners themselves. As troubles mounted in the late 1980s, Tex Schramm treated the losing on the field and economic misfortune as an aberration more than anything else. Seeing no reason to change, Schramm and the rest of the team's leadership triangle, including Coach Landry and player personnel director Gil Brandt, worked exactly the same way in early 1989 as they had for the past couple of decades.

Known for a reasonable demeanor and strong worth ethic—sometimes sleeping on the couch in his Valley Ranch office—Brandt was busy in the off-season getting ready for the draft, just as he had done for the Cowboys year after year. The notion that the Cowboys had no foreseeable way to pay its drafted stars in the future was treated with indifference. The situation could not be that bad, the thinking was, and even if it was nobody could do anything about it but keep working. The 1989 draft was forthcoming and Dallas had a first-round pick; the team needed a quarterback and a whole lot more.

In 1988, America's Team groveled in the cellar of the NFC's East Division, mustering just three paltry wins in a 16-game schedule. Running back Herschel Walker ran behind a patchwork offensive line on legs too tired after too many carries at the University of Georgia and professionally in the failed United States Football League. As a Cowboy in 1988, Walker rushed for more than 1,500 yards but was sent pounding into the line of scrimmage more than 360 times, yielding drudgery more than offensive efficiency. Spectators got the feeling, if they were paying attention at all, that the Dallas Cowboys were literally being run into the ground. Empty seats in Irving's Texas Stadium outnumbered those occupied at many of the home games. Fan interest was lethargic and waning.

The painful result was the Cowboys' third straight losing season, which followed a legendary 20-year run of winning years under Schramm and Landry, including the five Super Bowl appearances in the 1970s and 1980s. Tony Dorsett, the legendary Cowboys running back who was tough enough to take a head-on blow from an All-Pro linebacker but able to change direction so fluidly that defenders often did not realize he was going the other way, was long gone. So was quarterback Roger Staubach, the disciplined Navy graduate who almost never bristled under pressure in his heyday. The only holdover was Coach Landry, still prowling the sideline in 1988 in his trademark dark suit, hat perched on his head and addressing anyone from team members to the media in the same, even tones he spoke with since taking the job in 1960.

The Cowboys had changed, though, by early 1989, and so had the franchise's namesake city. It did not help the deteriorating plight of the team that the once raging, if not unreasonably robust Dallas economy, which bubbled up beginning in the late 1970s and early 1980s on the strength of oil, banking, and real estate while much of the nation suffered economic recession, was in total economic collapse. Unprecedented growth during the city's boom period, when available jobs, incomes, and the downtown skyline reached higher levels with each passing day, helped Dallas transform from an oversized, somewhat-refined oil and cow town into a vibrant, powerful American metropolis, with girth in banking, emerging technology, and oil.

Northern U.S. factories had idled in the late 1970s and early 1980s as recession and import pressures shifted economic growth and power south, toward Dallas's Sun Belt region. Dallas's housing market, as a direct result, soared. As business and real estate expanded quickly, funding came from the many new rapidly growing savings and loans that had sprung up throughout the area. Hosting the 1984 Republican National Convention at the downtown Reunion Arena was a shining moment for the city. Everything in Dallas, it appeared, had turned to gold.

Fortunes and fanfare would quickly decline, however, as the city's bubble economy burst. Longtime majority team owner Clint Murchison, once listed among the world's wealthiest men, had been forced to sell his beloved Cowboys and controlling interest in Irving's Texas Stadium to another oilman, Bright, in 1984 for $60 million following a protracted legal dispute over the Murchison estate after the death of Clint's brother John. The next year, Murchison would file one of America's most surprising bankruptcies. Bright, who bought the Cowboys at the age of 63 with a consortium of 11 minority owners, including Houston businessman Ed Smith, was a Texas A&M graduate who operated under the gentleman's principle that a handshake was legally binding and that wealth represented risks both taken and to be taken. Continuing the hands-off management style employed for decades by Murchison, Bright, a self-made millionaire oilman who reached wealthy status by 1950 and owned a part of more than 100 companies 20 years later, was more a Cowboys fan than leader, enjoying games from the solitude provided by a luxury suite. Bright focused daily on his Bright & Co. interests more than the fortunes of the Cowboys, checking in at Valley Ranch more on a periodic than regular basis. Tex Schramm maintained the biggest office at the Cowboys' complex; Bright was just looking for civic and social investment and a little football fun for his money.

From the looks of it, Bright and the minority owners in the consortium had done well with their $60 million. Shortly after he and the group bought the team, it moved into the new $20 million Cowboys Center in Valley Ranch, the facility started under Murchison's ownership. At Texas Stadium, the Cowboys unveiled more than 100 new luxury suites, giving the team more high-rent social boxes than any stadium in the country at the time. The Cowboys were respectable in 1985, Bright's first year of ownership, piecing together nine wins against seven losses, but missed the playoffs for only the second time in 19 years. Football woes were the least of Dallas's problems, however.

A savings and loan banking network that burgeoned beginning in the 1970s, feeding off a lack of institutional and governmental control and cozy relationships between oilmen and real estate developers, began to crumble. With little established government savings and loan oversight, lending had been lax throughout the region for years. High-rise commercial buildings and lavish houses were funded by banks backed largely by oil money. When crude prices plummeted due in part to excess export production by Saudi Arabia and Kuwait, prices fell below $10 per barrel on average. Years before, oil prices had been double and even triple that amount and thus the dramatic price fall sent shock waves through the crude-backed Dallas economy. As portfolios throughout Texas shriveled, banks flailed, struggling for survival. Bankruptcies on the personal and corporate level soared, reaching record highs.

Floor after floor of the once-booming office towers were quiet, in need of tenants. Commercial foreclosures in the Dallas area topped $1 billion. Crime was on the rise, posting double-digit increases from previous years. Housing starts were in decline, and thousands of new houses sat unsold, a record inventory that sent market prices sharply downward. The Federal Home Loan Bank Board stepped in, suspending deposit insurance for Texas savings and loan companies applying for state charters, in an effort to stop the weak lending practices. The damage, though, was already done.

Like many oil- and bank-based wealthy Texans, Bum Bright took a hard hit when Dallas's economic bubble rapidly deflated. He owned a significant share of First Republic Bank, a savings and loan that was, for a brief period at the peak of excess, the largest bank in Texas. He was also a majority owner of another S&L, Bright Banc Savings Association. Built on questionable real estate loans that took advantage of weak federal guidelines, both banks fell into deep trouble when property prices dropped quickly from previous historic highs. Compounding Bright's problems was another investment—his beloved Cowboys.

An unexpected losing season in 1986 was not just an aberration; it was becoming the norm for the once-proud Cowboys. Fan interest was dwindling and Landry and Schramm appeared to have lost their legendary magic. The franchise hit a particularly low point along with its league counterparts in 1987 when the NFL players union went on strike. League play was interrupted and team income took a direct hit. With picket-line-crossing substitute players standing in for the unionized stars for almost half the year, television ratings tumbled, as did team revenues, throughout the NFL. Attendance at Dallas games dropped by more than 15,000 fans per game on average, and souvenir and concession revenue dropped in accordance by more than one-third. The Cowboys lost again that year, winning just seven games against eight losses.

By 1988, Bright's investment in First Republic Bank became almost totally worthless as the institution failed. The 1 million shares he owned went from a value of $38 per share to $1. The man who owned 40 percent of the Dallas Cowboys and 100 percent of Texas Stadium's controlling authority was in financial shambles. At the time, the bank's collapse was the costliest end to a financial institution ever for American taxpayers, with a bailout tab exceeding $3 billion. That same year, the Cowboys hit another historic post–America's Team low, mustering just three wins as Herschel Walker pounded into the line of scrimmage almost 400 fan-numbing times. Franchise gross revenues for the year barely eclipsed $30 million and most of that came from league-distributed television dollars. Bright controlled Texas Stadium, but municipal law in Irving did not allow him to sell beer. Fans just brought in their own, brown-bagging by the ice-chest full, while Bright's Cowboys lost millions against team payroll and operation costs that exceeded $40 million. Dallas had earned the overall number one pick in the following year's draft with its dismal on-field showing in 1988, but America's Team was bleeding money, losing almost $1 million per month operationally, and in need of far more than just one promising new player.

Normally, loss-leading hobbies born of passion are something multimillionaires can rather easily overcome, but fortunes in Dallas for Bright, and oil and bank men like him, were heading south, fast. A single $10 million annual negative cash-flow vacuum, then, could not be overlooked. The Cowboys were in effect one of several wide-open drains on Bright's fast-sinking empire. The team's plush headquarters, appointed with soft blue carpeting and photos of championship teams, and a trio of experienced, well-heeled football men exuding success in presence alone was nothing more than comforting cover to the imbedded, prevailing Cowboys' frailty. The franchise had fallen in unison with Dallas's economy from proliferation to complete instability, and drastic changes were in immediate order. Financially desperate to avoid former owner Murchison's bankrupt plight, Bright placed his beloved Dallas Cowboys on the market for the sale price of $180 million. The news was reported in modest headlines around the country in January 1989.

New Day Dawning

The taste of the morning vacation hangover was not unfamiliar, but neither was it welcome on a sunny winter morning in Mexico's Cabo San Lucas, the small resort town located at the southern tip of the Baja California peninsula. His tongue was parched and clinging to the roof of his mouth, fighting against lingering flavors from the night before; his eyes rumbled in their sockets with the pain of a tiny pinch when they moved. Tequila has a way of doing that, luring victims with its romance of craft and ethnicity to stay for a seductive spell before delivering a hard, final parting punch that lasts deep into the next day.

Jerral W. "Jerry" Jones, 46 years old at the time, had fallen for the trick before. A risk-taking oil and gas man, he helped define in his younger days the "live hard, play hard" credo popular among businessmen who love finding the next million to be made just as they love catching the biggest fish or capping last call at the bar with the night's best story. So Jones knew the moment his eyes cracked open that morning in Cabo San Lucas he could not escape remnants of too much Mexican tequila; only time would restore his proper senses. He canceled the scheduled morning fishing trip, trading the swirling waters of the Pacific for a comfortable chair, a hot cup of coffee, and a morning paper. News of the day was mostly uneventful except for one small but nonetheless attention-getting blurb: Bum Bright's Dallas Cowboys were for sale.

To most people reading the story, the news was probably interesting at best, a passing trivial sporting tidbit. Bright, after all, was almost completely unknown as owner of the Cowboys, save some Texans who knew well the story of Clint Murchison's downfall. To Jerry Jones, though, news of the sale was fortuitous, the kind of too-good-to-be-true coincidence resulting in must-be-seized opportunity. Skipping the morning fishing trip and blearily picking up the newspaper, he went in two blinks of his weighty eyelids from groggy and regretful to glad he took a few too many shots of tequila the night before. Ten cups of freshly brewed java could not have jolted him as did this news that the Cowboys were for sale. Since his days as a football-playing, big-thinking college student, Jones wanted to own a professional football team. Twenty-five years of searching and dreaming was suddenly more real in possibility than any liquor-laced mirage.

Growing up as a small child in the then-rural cropland landscape far on the outskirts of the state capital of Little Rock, Arkansas, Jones lived in a future suburb decades from change that one longtime Jones friend characterizes as "North of North Little Rock." A landscape of cropland accented by small country stores and cousins living beside cousins, the community known officially as Rose City and nicknamed Dogtown was far from metropolitan, but it had just enough spillover impact from the nearby city to inspire hope in some. Born in October 1942, Jones was three years old when his father, J.W. "Pat" Jones, opened a fruit stand on a roadside buffered by acres and acres of agriculture fields near the family's Rose City home. Small in stature, standing just 5'6", Pat Jones possessed a large, likeable personality driven by the power of positive thinking. He almost always saw the proverbial glass half full, believing he would find a way to fill the other half even if it required hard work and nontraditional thinking. Bolstered by the success of the fruit stand, Pat decided to open the first supermarket in the area, borrowing the money despite friends who questioned the need for such a store.

Pat's Supermarket was a family business in the truest sense, involving Pat Jones, his wife, Arminta, and their two children, son Jerry and daughter Jacque. The family lived upstairs, above the store, and a young Jerry Jones greeted customers weekend mornings while wearing a black suit and bow tie. His mother worked in the store in every capacity imaginable.

"Everybody thought he [Pat] was crazy," Arminta Jones said. "But I want you to know, for the grand opening it was such a big blowout that the fire department had to come out and escort the traffic."

Anybody could sell a loaf of bread, but Pat Jones sought to make the experience of buying a loaf of bread entertaining, separating his store from others in the region. He died in 1997, two years after open-heart surgery, ending a lifelong relationship between Jerry and his father that often leaned more toward brotherly friendship than a father-son dynamic. The impact Pat Jones had on his son beginning in those early days is obvious. Sitting in his office more than 50 years later, Jerry recalls how his father was one of the first to make his supermarket a place for one-stop household shopping, incorporating such items as toothpaste and pots and pans in his grocery-based retail store. Such diversified supermarkets were not commonplace in those days. Having the most impact on Jerry, though, was how his father made entertainment a part of the shopping experience, translating enthusiasm and marketing creativity into recognized and productive retail flair.

A storyteller who delivered a firm handshake with colloquial warmth, Pat Jones was known to greet guests on weekends at his store wearing a white cowboy suit accented with "boots and all." He built a radio broadcast area in the store for live shows, hiring a top personality from the area, Brother Hal. Known for hosting offbeat on-air talent shows including everything from dogs doing tricks to little girls singing, Brother Hal was a Memphis native who first made his mark in Arkansas on the air with a trademark nasal, southern twang. Jerry Jones says he learned through his father the value of promotion in business.

"From Dad's store, Brother Hal conducted live shows on Arkansas's KLRA radio station while people were shopping and buying groceries," said Jones. "And Dad was visible in the store. He became a personality, a figure. He gave the customer added value; something other than just a can of beans."

As a teenager, living large in the land where young men learned to drive by the age of 12 and owned a shotgun before that, Jones stocked shelves and sacked groceries at his father's flagship market during summers and on weekends. Jones loved hunting, bird hunting in particular, making use of land acquired by his father through business success, but his purest passion was football, and he starred as a running back at North Little Rock High School. Some pundits have described Jones and his family as being from the wrong side of the tracks during this period, but that is not necessarily true. Nearby Little Rock certainly had its wealth and tradition and yes, the Joneses were removed from those social circles that relied more on reformed southern gentility than a rural, shoot-at-first-sight mentality, but this was Arkansas in the 1950s and 1960s. Manhattan or downtown Dallas, it was not.

Almost everybody from the more rural reaches of the Natural State, including President Bill Clinton and the late football coach Bear Bryant, started from scratch in similar backgrounds. The croplands of North Little Rock were no different from most of the rest of the state. Rural in nature, the dialect featured syllables that often got lost and the letter G had no place in verbalized word endings, as in, "we were blowin' and goin'" or "we were kickin' their butts." Few residents needed a lawyer, as deals were made on handshakes. A man's honor relied on keeping his word to the smallest detail.

Pat Jones's business grew and eventually his first supermarket became a small chain of stores scattered throughout northern and central Arkansas. With profits and creative leverage, he bought an insurance company in the Ozark Mountains, Springfield, Missouri-based Modern Security Life Insurance Company. A nonstop worker who enjoyed warm conversation and cold drink and was not satisfied with sitting still unless it was during an early-morning hunt, Pat Jones parlayed his first fruit stand into a sizable estate, considering the humble beginnings, by the time Jerry Jones was in high school.

"My dad once said, 'I knew I was never going to be a millionaire, so I just decided to try to borrow a million,'" Jones recalls.

As a senior in high school, Jones was the toast of the town with a moderately wealthy, well-known family and a gridiron persona in a football-crazed region. In 1960, just one team in the state played Division I college football: the University of Arkansas at Fayetteville. Coached by Frank Broyles, the national championship–contending member of the Southwest Conference had the entire state under its spell. Outside of Razorback football, which nearly everyone followed fervently, smaller cities and towns like North Little Rock rallied around high school teams. On fall Friday nights, nobody was home because they were all at the local prep game, while on fall Saturday nights, everybody was home, gathered around the radio listening to Arkansas play.

A hard-nosed competitor, Jones was not blessed with the greatest on-field speed. He was quick and feisty and given the ball to carry because of an unmistakable drive to get the extra yard for the first down or get to the end zone for a score. When Jones signed a scholarship to play in college for Coach Broyles, he saw it as the ultimate achievement considering most of the state was enamored with the red-and-white Razorbacks to the point of obsession. Broyles, who would later become a close friend of Jones's, recruited the southwest region around Arkansas the way a discerning shopper works the produce aisle at market: the best were chosen and easily collected at will. Playing for the Razorbacks was a privilege, not a decision.

In Fayetteville, Jones was a standout from the moment he arrived, and not just on the football field. He drove a Cadillac Eldorado and wore a big smile and a diamond pinkie ring. Among classmates he met on his first day at the Fayetteville campus was Gene Chambers, an athletic beauty who made 18 straight free throws in the state championship basketball game in high school. As a college student at Arkansas, she had a firm foundation. Her family was well established in banking in Arkansas and she was crowned as a teen Miss Arkansas USA and Poultry Princess. Her roommate and sorority sister on campus was the future first wife of another of Jones's classmates, Jimmy Johnson.

The football field and accompanying environment at Arkansas was Jones's primary residence, as high demands were placed on Broyles's well-coached and talented squads. On the freshman team, Jones was coached by the young upstart Barry Switzer. Jones was moved to guard because he was too slow for running back, and his feistiness and hypercompetitive drive served him well in the trenches. As an upperclassman, he was a varsity starter, effectively moving bigger defensive linemen with his 180-pound frame through determination and will. Lessons learned by Jones as a Razorback remain with the team owner and general manager today to the point that they emerge in applicable football and life stories more frequently than not. Knowing Jerry Jones is recognizing that the years he spent at the University of Arkansas are structurally embedded in his foundation. Some stories are more serious than others, but all have their merits.

During his sophomore season, a year the Razorbacks reached the Sugar Bowl in New Orleans, the team was staying on the Mississippi Gulf Coast the night before the game. Jones roomed with Jimmy Johnson both in the dorm and in the hotel room for road games, and the night before the game against the University of Mississippi the duo decided that curfew came a little too early. Neither had traveled much by that point and they wanted to experience some local flavor while spending the night on the Gulf Coast.

Staying in Biloxi, Jones and Johnson were in their room in time for lights-out but left soon after for a nearby oyster bar, ordering a dozen oysters on the half shell and a couple of soda pops. Midway through the devious delight, a hand hit their shoulders. Jones and Johnson turned around, finding Arkansas assistant coach Doug Dickey standing over them.

"Scared wasn't the word for it," Jones said. "I had tears in my eyes. I knew I was fixin' to go home."

Dickey told the Arkansas players to get quickly back to their room and not tell a soul about what happened. They obeyed the coach, returning quietly to their room, and played against Ole Miss the next day. The Razorbacks lost the 1963 game 17–13, but they returned most starters from the team the next year and appeared poised for a national championship run in Jones's junior season. But it would not turn out that way. It is from this experience in his junior and senior seasons that Jones formed one of his favorite recitations about winning, losing, and the bounce of the ball.

Many pundits predicted Arkansas had enough talent to take the 1963 national championship, yet fate had a different idea as every call and every morsel of fortune went the other way. The highly praised Razorbacks earned just five wins against five losses. The loss deficit combined totaled just 23 points.

Only one Arkansas player made the All-Southwest Conference team announced at the end of the season. Recalls Jones, "Everybody said, 'Well, they did not have the talent. They were overrated.' We came back the next season, adding just one new player. We [played] against Tulsa, a very good team. They took a 14–0 lead on us, but we came back to win a close game. Everything looked just like the [close] games the year before, but this time we won.

"Then we went down to Texas to play the No. 1 team in the country. [Texas head coach] Darrell Royal went for two late in the game and a player dropped a pass in the end zone, giving us the win."

Jones says he and teammates looked in the proverbial mirror, amazed and amused that they could beat the No. 1 team. They began to believe that they could compete on the national level and that the year before was more fluke than foretelling of fortunes. The Razorbacks were not scored on again until the Cotton Bowl and went on to an undefeated season, claiming a national championship.

"Everybody said, 'Well, they should have won, because they had all that talent!'" Jones says. "Confidence is such a part of winning. It takes talent, of course. You have to be well-coached and prepared. But I learned that season you have to believe you are the best."

He was named a co-captain of the 1964 team because of his leadership and camaraderie with teammates, an honor he still touts as a lifetime highlight. Weighing just 182 pounds as a lineman in Arkansas's 10–7 Cotton Bowl win over Nebraska, Jones was not a professional football prospect. He had a better opportunity anyway. Jerry Jones was a natural born businessman. As a student, he had hustled tickets before games, sold shoes from the trunk of his car, and during a redshirt year ran a taxi service, shuttling rich fans from the airport to the stadium and back for money. Married to Gene during his senior year and therefore ready for a job at graduation, he fortunately had a father who believed a young man should not be limited in opportunity by age. The family had a business and the business had a place for Jerry. Right after graduation, Jones went to work recruiting insurances sales agents twice his age to work for Modern Security Life Insurance Company.

A place in the family business was a natural and a given. No outside apprenticeships first for Jerry Jones. Pat Jones and his son were like best friends or brothers, able to travel together, hunt together, and share a beer together, but Pat also made his son a full-fledged, empowered business partner the moment he graduated from Arkansas. Jones would later earn a master's degree in business administration (MBA), but he says his real education came in the business world in his twenties. Jerry and wife Gene moved to Missouri, where he assumed the title of executive vice president of the family's insurance company. The business fit well considering Jones is the consummate salesman and motivator, though it hardly satisfied his insatiable think-big appetite. Jones was seeking multiple business opportunities on the side from his first day on the job. One monthly paycheck was just not enough to fund dreams the size he was dreaming. Jones bought Shakey's Pizza franchise rights for the area around Springfield and purchased real estate there as well, seeking to make his first million by the time he was 25. Debt incurred in the purchases got him closer to broke than wealthy, however, and his survival in the business world was in jeopardy due to too much debt against too little cash flow.

In Jones's view, the insurance company was a chip, one that could be cashed in for something much, much larger. For many people, the job at the insurance company and wealth from his wife's side of the family would have been enough, but the newlyweds had their sights set on more. With firstborn child Stephen, a toddler, at home, Jerry was gone more than not, working long hours during the week and attending late-night business dinners and hunting and partying with friends on the weekends. He was branching out in business, taking on heavy debt to finance a multitude of ventures that would eventually include poultry and local TV stations. Pat and Arminta Jones had taught Jerry how to build something from nothing on the backbone of leverage but did not always share their son's ambition to so quickly parlay assets. Pat lectured him on his fast-paced, risking style, suggesting time with children is precious.

Take advantage of the opportunity, he said. Or else have regrets later.

"You're going to wake up one of these days, and you're going to be sitting across the table from a 22-year-old just like you," Pat Jones told his son. "The reason I know that is because it happened to me."

Jones missed the chivalrous glamour and competitive camaraderie of football so much that in 1965, one year after graduating college and barely into his new job, he traveled to Miami just after Joe Robbie bought the AFL's Miami Dolphins franchise to see if he could talk his way into a minority ownership position. Jones knew he was not big enough to play professional football, but he believed he had the capacity to own part of a team and be involved with it, making significant contributions. Robbie met with Jones, talking with him and team head coach George Wilson as they moved furniture into the administrative offices.

"Do you mind lending a hand?" Robbie asked Jones, who helped the Dolphin duo move a desk into the owner's new office.

Robbie had no ownership opportunity for Jones, but he did have many answers to the young man's numerous questions about the league and its operational structure. Jones, for instance, asked detailed questions about the team/stadium relationship and began to envision revenue possibilities off the playing field. In hindsight, the trip to Miami was hardly a waste of time.

The next year, Jones made a telephone call to another AFL team owner. This time he was trying to secure majority ownership of a team despite the fact that he was just 23 years old and without a strong cash position for leverage. Jones, in fact, was earning a salary at the family business of not much more than $1,000 per month. Barron Hilton, the grandfather of Paris Hilton, was selling the San Diego Chargers. Jones called Hilton for a meeting, saying he wanted to buy the team. Hilton agreed to meet with Jones, telling him the $5.8 million price tag and that he sure looked young. Jones cobbled together an ambitious if not slightly unrealistic financing plan with a labor union to get the deal done. He was about to pull the trigger before the debt scared him off. He had been stressed under the weight of borrowing to buy the land and pizza franchises, and more than $5 million seemed awfully imposing when it came time to sign on the dotted line. Plus, his father was not so supportive. Ultimately, Hilton sold the team to another buyer, but the opportunity had only whetted his insatiable football appetite for more.

With Jerry and Gene supporting a young family of five—daughter Charlotte was the Joneses' second born, while son Jerry Jr. was born in 1969—and a hunger for the type of wealth that allows holders to buy premier professional sports franchises, the family's insurance company was sold, ending the father-son business partnership. The move was significant for Jerry because his previous business ventures were based completely on his ability to borrow against his insurance company ownership. Proceeds from the sale were not enough for Jones to buy an NFL team, but he had other ideas. He sought to parlay his worth into the highest payoff business he knew—oil and gas exploration. Investing heavily in Oklahoma, Jones went primarily after land for drilling that previously had promise but that had been abandoned after coming up dry for others. Some were held by big oil companies that had spent millions drilling deep, only to abandon amid too many disappointing dry holes. Jones leased land from the oil companies, drilling between dry holes and striking a fortunate 12 of his first 13 starts.

By the 1980s, he and a business partner had founded an oil and gas company under the trade name Arkoma. Based in Little Rock, the business would make Jones very wealthy, considering some strikes made by the company yielded $50 million to $80 million or more. In hindsight, it all looks so easy, parlaying modest wealth into millions in just more than a decade. One cannot forget, though, that the risk Jones took was enormous, and hundreds of thousands of dollars or more was needed for each drilling site. More often than not such dice rolls in business yield dry holes and failure over fortune. To become an NFL team owner like Robbie or Hilton, however, Jones needed cash, so he put his money on the line, went looking for tomorrow's fortune, and got a little bit lucky along the way.

Says Jones, "I am a risk taker. That's why the people who are making the plays are making the play calls."

A famous tale of Jones and his entry into the oil and gas business involves an initial meeting with a geologist who told Jones if he spent $3 million and "drilled right there" he would find oil. "If you're so sure," Jones responded, "why don't you invest your money?" That is the type of cynicism Jones blended with optimism to balance risk with calculation. In the end, it worked out better than all right. As an oilman, Jones traveled frequently to Dallas for meetings, making the five-hour, one-way drive from Little Rock, where he and his family had resettled after the sale of their insurance company. Since the 1970s Dallas had been the nerve center of America's oil and gas trade, and Jones enjoyed the bigger environment and faster-paced business style.

Jones lived large like any wealthy businessman of the era, wining and dining appropriately, but he never lost his sense of frugality and value, friends and family say. An expensive dinner was never a problem if it was deserving or beneficial. Something like an overzealous electric bill, however, might get his attention for its wastefulness. Weekdays, he traveled and ran the business while his children attended private schools in Little Rock; each was a standout student. Weekends, he was outdoors fishing or hunting or, in the late winter, attending horse races in nearby Hot Springs, Arkansas. The next big strike, he figured, was around the corner just like the next largemouth bass. He needed only to navigate appropriately through the lily pads, tossing a lure in just the right spot.

Jones would later say he was driven to such risk taking because making money is "like trying to quench a thirst." No amount he ever made, he says, even an $80 million oil strike, satisfied the thirst. "I've never gone to sleep a night yet," said Jones, referring to money making, "without wanting something more to drink."

Life in Little Rock in the late 1970s and 1980s was good for the Jones family, who lived in the suburban Pleasant Valley neighborhood, built around a lush country club and golf course. Jones coached his oldest son's youth team, and by the time Stephen was a star quarterback at Catholic High School, Jerry was so hands-on with his football he moved his office so he could overlook the team's practice field while working. Jones kept binoculars on his desk so that he could closely appraise the action. Away from the office, Jones was known to call his secretary afternoons during the season for field reports. An excellent student with high test scores, Stephen could have attended college just about anywhere when he left Catholic. He was accepted into Princeton but signed with Arkansas to play football because, like his father, he was always a Razorback at heart. He majored in chemical engineering—the only player on the team to do so—because Jones had made a deal with his son.

"I told him if he went to Arkansas [over Princeton], he had to take the hardest curriculum [the school offered]," Jones says.

On the field for Arkansas head coach Ken Hatfield, Stephen was a linebacker. Off the field, he was an exemplary student. Excellence in academics and achievement is a Jones family expectation. Charlotte did well in school. So did Jerry Jr., who received a law degree from Georgetown University. Friends say the family was living the American dream in many ways in Little Rock, socializing regularly with friends, taking trips to the beach, enjoying private hunting lodges and land, and spending long weekends in Mexico. For Jones, though, none of it was enough with his one great temptation unsatisfied. Even though in business Jones had for years been "goin' and blowin', rollin' it and movin' it," he was not satisfied.

Restless, Jones could not find the reward from competition in traditional business that he found on the football field, both in high school and in college. An oil strike delivers a rush and cause for opening a $1,000 bottle of champagne, but the thrill and challenge quickly pass. In football, the goal line is hard to reach and the opponent constantly changes in both uniform and strategy, making the game for Jones an effective quench for his insatiable competitive thirst. Instinct said he needed a team, but finding one presented quite a challenge since owners of NFL franchises historically sell only in rare, necessary instances, not to mention the financing problem when teams are available or the requisite speed needed in beating other potential suitors to the table. The United States has more than a few multimillionaires interested in owning a professional sports team.

That is why Jones felt in his tequila-strained heart that morning in Mexico that fate had delivered him a favor. His mouth was entirely too dry, his warm blue eyes achingly bloodshot, and his firm hands unsteady. Yet Jones's well-known optimism was firmly in place after he picked up the morning newspaper.

The Dallas Cowboys were for sale!

From Mexico, Jones telephoned Bum Bright at his Bright & Co. office in Texas. His voice gravelly reverberating in deep, rough tones, a reminder of too many drinks and too little quality sleep the night before, Jones did not hide his hangover from Bright. Neither did he hide his desire to buy the team.

"Now I think I'm going to die," Jones told Bright, "but if I live, I'm going to come back to buy the Dallas Cowboys."

Bright was asking $180 million total for both the Cowboys and stadium control rights that extended for another 20 years. Jones's net worth at the time was just about that, or slightly less, depending on oil and gas future earnings calculations. In Dallas's finance-averse environment of 1989, buying the team was more difficult than it might have been at any other time. A net worth of $180 million was barely enough. Donald Carter, who owned the NBA's Dallas Mavericks, was bidding for the team. So was minority owner Ed Smith, who owned 27 percent of the Cowboys with Bright but was unable to get needed money together for the purchase.

Determined—"The Cowboys were my devil," he says—Jones moved fast, piecing together the deal Bright said would get it done. Keeping Smith as a minority owner, he also brought in Charles Wyly, Sam Wyly, and Evan Wyly, affiliated with the Bonanza Steakhouse chain, leaving him with a controlling 63 percent (Jones would quickly buy out his partners, though). To get $140 million in financing to purchase the team and the stadium rights, he had to make personal guarantees in excess of $80 million to banks and the limited partners, pledging future oil and gas royalties. To get the team, he leveraged much of everything the family had, borrowing $40 million from a Texas bank and other amounts from individuals and elsewhere to finance his purchase.

Jones says in today's business climate he could put together a $2 billion deal with that type of down payment, but times in Dallas in 1989 were completely different.

Wanting to keep his interest in buying the team out of the news, Jones asked Schramm to sign a confidentiality agreement on behalf of the organization while he conducted due diligence. Keeping Schramm quiet was not easy—the man was a professional sports public relations wizard of his day, well connected and overtly friendly with most Cowboys beat journalists. Similarly, Jones had a big family in Arkansas, with cousins and nephews who learned he was in legitimate pursuit of the purchase. The news leaked to a Dallas television station, which reported the story. A decade later, Bright blamed the breach on Jones's nephew, saying he had told friends in Arkansas his uncle was buying the Cowboys. One of the nephew's friends supposedly had a father who was an executive at a local television affiliate and the secret got out. Jones says he does not know how the story broke, but he remembers being shocked by the result. In an instant he went from being a regionally recognized businessman to a leading national story.

Before the story broke, Jones quietly researched the team and the NFL from an exploratory business perspective, reading Herschel Walker's multipage employment contract and traveling to San Francisco to meet with 49ers head coach Bill Walsh and team general manager John McVay for hours, asking dozens of questions about how an NFL team should be properly operated. Jones also went to New York, meeting with then–ABC president Dan Burke to learn about television networks and the relationship with the league. Jones wanted to expose all angles of the payoff, proving potential would support the incredible risk.

"Burke told me," says Jones, "you could have 2,000 producers in Hollywood working on the perfect script, but there is no way to capture the soap opera effect of what goes on around the NFL game during the week. No way to capture that."

Ultimately, Jones wanted ownership of the Dallas Cowboys so badly it did not matter what anybody said. He had to have the franchise at any cost. Money had been plentiful, but it was no good if it could not buy the one thing he wanted. He was pleased, though, that research revealed to him the Cowboys and other NFL teams were leaving considerable potential revenue streams untapped. So he moved forward, fast.

Jones was surprised, to say the least, when he sat down one-on-one with Bright in Dallas to outline terms of the sale and found dozens of media members covering the story were waiting outside for any news to report. The once-quiet story had inspired a full-scale media frenzy after the first article announced his interest. Schramm, the consummate PR man, delivered negotiation updates to journalists in ticker-tape fashion. Bright hated to let the team go, but he was overextended with the banking and oil slumps. He needed to make the sale, and Jones was willing to pay something close to his price and get the deal done quickly.

With oversized glasses that shadowed his thin, aging face, Bright never lost his sense of humor or his sense of what the Cowboys were worth. Negotiating in his office with Jones, he sealed the deal with a handshake, solidifying terms that turned out to be the highest sale price ever at the time for an NFL team on a single, legal-size sheet of paper. Jones and Bright had stalemated in negotiation over a final $300,000, deciding to settle the difference as oilmen would—with the flip of a coin. Jones got the honors of the flip and the customary in-air call.

"Tails," said Jones as the coin sped from his finger toward the ceiling, where it pinged with force, ricocheting against a wall before landing in an ashtray.

Amused, Bright remained seated, waiting for the result.

Jones walked over for a look.

"Heads," he said, grinning.

Bright got the $300,000 difference, but Jones was hardly disappointed.

Even though another bidder later tried to raise the price by $10 million before Jones could formally close the deal, Bright kept his handshake promise, putting the Arkansas oilman on the path to owning his NFL dream team. Outside, the media had created a circus atmosphere. Inside, however, the moment was a relatively quiet one among businessmen. Both Jones and Bright maintained somewhat solemn faces, hiding immense internal enthusiasm. Jones was getting the team; Bright was getting out of trouble.

But from that handshake on, neither the franchise nor the league would ever be the same.

Pressure Creates Coverage

"I had played the game.
Plus, I had the confidence
that someone like me [from
a small town in Arkansas]
could do something big."

—*Jerry Jones*

2

Pressure Creates Coverage

Regret does not fit easily into the vocabulary of Jerry Jones. He's a self-described optimist who naturally wakes up some days with doubt but has purged it by the time he's out of a morning shower, well before reaching the office. He admits mistakes, often rather easily, but incorporates those into building blocks for focused opportunity rather than dwelling on them. Take, for instance, his quick firing of Tom Landry immediately after reaching a deal to buy the team, an event that remains two decades and dozens of major actions later a signature if not defining moment for Jones as an NFL owner.

In Jones's mind, he and Bright had a deal from the moment they shook hands and that was good enough to immediately make changes. The deal between Jones and Bright was announced publicly at a joint-party press conference on February 25, 1989, but the NFL had not officially approved the transaction and would not do so until its owners meeting scheduled for two months later. Some people would have waited for league approval, but Jones knew he had given his word and Bright had given his, all but assuring he was the league's newest owner. In business dealings in the past Jones had had only one major handshake agreement go awry when the other party had a change of heart. This was not an agreement he planned to let get away. The more immediate ownership he took, the more the team would truly be his. And he did not think the beleaguered franchise could wait on change. For his big investment to pay off, the ailing Cowboys franchise needed change yesterday.

Once he shook hands, Jones went about the tasks of ownership. In no time, he had a Dallas Cowboys helmet painted on the tail of his personal Lear 35A jet. In even less time, just half a day after shaking Bright's hand, he was traveling with Schramm to Austin, Texas, to see Landry about a little employment matter. The story has been told over the years so many times Jones does not spend much time recounting the details. What he does offer is historical perspective and reflection. "Traumatic" is how Jones recalls the incident today; a building block of learning and opportunity the size of Texas Stadium. He did not know Landry, but he respected him as a fan the same way everybody who had watched the NFL since 1960 respected him. But after 29 years, Jones thought the coach was well past his prime and a change seemed overdue. Dallas desperately needed new direction for the sake of both the players and the fans. Another stoic season of Herschel Walker left and Herschel Walker right as Landry peered unemotionally from beneath his hat might drive many remaining fans totally and fatally away.

Bright was on board with Jones. He had been internally critical of Landry as head coach and Landry knew it to the point that he avoided discussion with Bright whenever possible. Bright knew from their private discussions that Jones was going to let Landry go. He even offered to do the dirty work himself, hinting later he would have done it anyway had the team remained his.

"[Change] happens in every business," Bright said at the time.

Recognizing Landry's father-figure popularity with fans, Jones had consulted two public relations firms on how to handle the termination. Each of the firms, one based in Texas and one in Washington, D.C., gave the very same recommendation: handle Landry's firing yourself, which was fine with Jones.

"I wanted to be a stand-up guy," he says. "Do it myself. I felt I was not a man if I did not go down there and do it myself. And my gut was telling me I needed to have personal dialogue with Coach Landry."

On the trip to Austin, where Landry had a vacation home, Jones praised Schramm for how he had built the Dallas football franchise from a fledgling startup in 1959 into a world-recognized brand. He noted how Schramm worked to get Dallas into the NFC East Division so the franchise could be on television in large, East Coast markets including New York and Philadelphia. And he bragged on Schramm's brilliance in creating strong tradition with tools like the famed Ring of Honor, which lines the interior of Texas Stadium, and how Schramm in general made the franchise and the game "bigger than life." Jones meant every word he said, certainly, but he was laying on the accolades because he could see how nervous Schramm was during the short trip to see Landry. Even so, the effervescent but visibly shaken Schramm was able to quip.

"Yeah," he said in response to Jones, "this would be a good business if you didn't have to play those games on Sunday."

The story is one Jones has told time and time again for two decades. Likely, he says, the chuckle is memorable because it was the highlight of an otherwise miserable day. The rest of the trip he would rather forget: hailing Landry from the golf course for the meeting; telling him face to face he would be replaced as coach and only getting cold, terse responses in return. Jones tried best as he could to offer Landry another position with the team, but the coach was not interested. Landry, fighting emotion and a bad cold, accepted the news with few words, giving Jones no relief from his obvious discomfort during the face-to-face meeting.

In all his years as a businessman, Jones had never personally fired a key employee. His first day as owner of the Cowboys—no, before he even officially owned the Cowboys—he was firing one of the most legendary coaches in the history of professional football; the man who guided Dallas to 20 consecutive winning seasons and had more career wins (270) than any NFL coach but George Halas and Don Shula. Landry, who died of leukemia in 2000 and never coached again after Jones let him go, did not take the firing well and neither did Schramm, who visibly choked up when discussing the termination at a press conference later that night. That, however, was nothing compared to the public outcry that followed the announcement of Landry's termination.

A giddy Jones, who was finally realizing his dream of owning a professional team, and the Dallas Cowboys no less, said at the press conference formally announcing the sale just hours after meeting with

Landry that buying the team was like Christmas for him. Within the next few sentences the media was officially told that, yes, rumors were correct: Landry was being terminated. Jones came off cold-hearted and insensitive. The media lashed out in response and so did fans. Sports talk radio was barely in play at the time, but that did not stop a firestorm of negativity that extended far beyond Texas. *The Dallas Morning News* ran a front page headline referring to a quote by NFL commissioner Pete Rozelle that said Landry's firing was similar to the death of former coaching great Vince Lombardi. The headline read: "Rozelle: 'This Is like Lombardi's Death.'"

Talk about pressure. The man one day removed from making a verbal agreement to join the NFL is accused by the league's well-respected commissioner in headlines of an act similar to killing Vince Lombardi. In hindsight, reflecting while sitting behind the desk of his Valley Ranch Cowboys office, once occupied by Schramm, Jones says he was simply ill-prepared for the firestorm, overcome with the thrill of buying the team and the difficulty of making drastic transition in a short period. He grades himself an "F" on handling of the matter and says he "didn't do a very good job" with the situation. Discussing it, Jones leans forward. Dressed in a trademark blue suit with his black cowboy boot–clad feet tightly crossed, he is tense, almost emotional. He did not see it coming. He had no idea how bad it would be. He should not, he says, have announced the purchase at the same time he announced Landry was terminated.

"The only thing that got me through it was the sheer enthusiasm of, 'I'm in the NFL,'" Jones says.

His optimism in light of the criticism was primed by the fact that Jones felt he had nabbed the perfect coach for his new team: Jimmy Johnson, his old college roommate from Arkansas who had won a national championship as a head coach at the University of Miami. Like his initial deal with Bright, their agreement was just verbal, but Johnson had agreed to take the head coaching job in Dallas; thus, Jones did not see any reason to give Landry an obligatory 30th-season victory lap, delaying the inevitable. Jones is typically short on patience when his sights are set on a goal. If he does not think a coach, or a particular employee, is right for the job, why wait? So he gave Landry notice and a $1 million contract buyout, money the financially struggling team could barely afford.

"I'm here and Jimmy's here," Jones told Landry when they met that fateful day.

Jones and Johnson were not the best buddies some portrayed them to be when it was announced the duo was uniting in Dallas. They had been teammates and roommates in college and Jerry's wife, Gene, had been sorority sisters with Jimmy's first wife in college, so assumptions were natural. They were close, yes, but not like brothers; more like two people who spent a lot of time together over the years and shared a passion for winning. Jones took notice when his old coach turned athletic director, Frank Broyles, did not try hard to hire then–Oklahoma State head coach Johnson to lead Arkansas when the school had an opening in 1984, opting instead for Air Force's Ken Hatfield. And Jones and Johnson had not remained in the closest of touch over the years. But Jones knew enough about Johnson to know that football was his life. Not family. Not hobbies. Football. After coaching five seasons at Miami, Johnson and his first wife divorced. His reputation was a well-earned football first, everything else in life tied for a distant second. Jones knew Johnson would work every waking moment to make the Cowboys winners again in the shortest time possible.

Landing the coach was the easy part, though. Johnson had known Jones for decades, since they were 18-year-old swaggering freshmen in Fayetteville. The public outside of Arkansas was just getting to know and understand Jerry Jones, Dallas Cowboys owner, and the early acquaintance was not going so well after the Landry dismissal. The challenge of Landry's popularity was complicated by his enthusiasm and the fact that over several decades nothing much had ever changed with the organization besides quarterbacks, going from, say, Roger Staubach to longtime backup Danny White.

At the initial press conference, Jones said he would be responsible for everything in the Dallas organization down to "socks and jocks." Jones meant he would be a hands-on owner, concerned with every aspect of the franchise, but his colloquialisms were easy targets.

Columnists, including Frank Luksa and Skip Bayless of the now-extinct *Dallas Times Herald*, suggested Jones was a hick from Arkansas who descended upon the Cowboys, uninvited. Bayless, in fact, called Jones in print an Arkansas "thrillbilly" for his freewheeling Arkansas dialect and ways.

Jones never questioned whether he could run the team amid the controversy. He had no experience with professional football. He noted he did not know how to draft players or when to schedule minicamps. He was "a little above ground zero in understanding shoulder pads and helmets, but not too far," and not too far "above ground zero in the area of TV and networks and things like that," but he had plenty of experience in business and assumed the learning curve could not be more than a few years of hard work. "Trading, draft picks…I had spent my entire life trading, trying to gain advantage in the transaction," Jones says years later in reflection. "I was doing real business in school and right after school while most my age were in apprenticeships. When I was 23 and 24 [years of age], I was facing some big financial challenges. Those were the basis of my education. I had taken on too much debt and had too much on my plate. I was on the high wire with no net."

His first days on the job with the Dallas Cowboys could easily have been described the very same way.

Working to Overcome Ills

A bit of a thrillbilly himself if the description fit Jones, Johnson, with his coiffed hair, southern-flavored dialect, and unrestrained wit, was so eager to move to the NFL and the Dallas Cowboys in particular that he left his head coaching job at Miami and joined Jones in Dallas without a contract. For almost one month he labored on nothing more than trust, working closely with Jones, preparing for the upcoming draft and learning about the team's available talent pool. Jones was so busy battling repercussions from the Landry firing, analyzing the franchise's personnel, preparing for the impending league approval vote, and crunching cash flow needs, not to mention needs for the upcoming draft, Johnson's contract could wait. And Johnson was so busy learning personnel, evaluating talent needs, and learning the ins-and-outs of the NFL, he too felt the contract could wait. Eventually, on his own accord, Jones presented Johnson with a contract, offering him a 10-year deal with one of the highest salaries in the league at more than $1 million per season.

"He [Johnson] did not ask for it," recalls Jones. "I gave it [the 10-year deal] to him gratuitously and I personally guaranteed it. Landry had been here for 29 years. I was guessing Jimmy would be here for 29 years."

But while the contract was generous in terms of dollars and years, the document did not give Johnson the ability to build the roster through draft picks and free agents. As the owner, Jones wanted full roster control and thus, says Jones, "Jimmy never had the authority to make one draft pick." Johnson, as other coaches working for the Cowboys after Jones bought the team, did not even have final say over the team's final 53-man roster. Jones, of course, offered Johnson plenty of input, just as he has every coach during his tenure. He has the control, but decisions are made "with the coaches, of course." That was initially fine with Johnson, who went immediately to work in his new job with Jones, Schramm, and Gil Brandt, who had made every Cowboys draft choice since 1960.

Jones, meanwhile, explained himself and his actions at every public appearance. Before the Arkansas state legislature, which commended its native son on purchasing the Cowboys, he apologized for appearing insensitive to Landry and, oh, by the way, he had received two death threats because of it. The pressure was intense and it had Jones's attention.

"I've been scared for the last 60 days," he said in April 1989, almost two months after making the deal to buy the team, "and I will remain scared. I want to make the right decisions every day. I want to be a great owner."

The best news of the emotionally draining spring for Jones came before the draft when NFL owners unanimously approved his application for ownership. The vote did not come easy, as anyone could have predicted. Hugh Culverhouse, owner of the Tampa Bay Buccaneers, wanted to know how Landry was fired when Jones was not yet officially approved by the NFL as an owner.

"He [Culverhouse] asked me, 'Under what authority have you made these changes?'" says Jones. "But I had a deal to buy the team. I said in effect Tex Schramm has made them. He was [team] president. He was there with me."

Despite the concern of Culverhouse and other owners, the NFL did approve Jones's application for ownership on April 18, 1989, at 11:05 AM in New York, making the 46-year-old Jones the third owner in the Cowboys' history. He left the meeting with a smiling Pete Rozelle and was pictured with his right fist clenched, pumping jubilantly in the air.

"It's great to be a Cowboy," he said. "My family has moved to Dallas. The rest of my life will be spent with the Dallas Cowboys on a day-to-day basis."

Jones was officially in. Unofficially, however, he was nowhere close. Joining a league under the control of longtime, more conservative owners like Wellington Mara of the New York Giants, Jones was seen as a potentially dangerous renegade, capable of bringing shame to a well-established organization. And even though they approved Jones, the league quickly established what came to be known as the "Jerry Jones rule," which limits tinkering that can be done with a franchise before the league approves ownership.

To learn quickly about the league and to get fellow owners on his side, Jones met when he could with Mara and owners Lamar Hunt of the Kansas City Chiefs, Art Modell of the Cleveland Browns, and Tom Benson of the New Orleans Saints, asking as many questions as they would answer. He said Modell was a hero of his in college for his hands-on approach to ownership and he sought to steal some plays from his playbook. But while the worst seemed to be over for Jones and the new-era Cowboys with the league's stamp of approval and Landry's firing months in arrears, reality had a totally different spin. Tex Schramm quit as the Cowboys president and general manager, selling his 3 percent of team ownership to Jones. Schramm became president of the NFL's new international league at the time, and Jones announced that he would become team general manager and president. There was really no room for Schramm, anyway; his departure was just a matter of finding the right opportunity. Nor was there room for Brandt, let go by Jones shortly after Schramm departed, or former team vice president of administration Joe Bailey, or a dozen or more other longtime Dallas Cowboys employees who had no place on Jerry's team. The Cowboys were all but broke and Jones had leveraged almost everything he had to get the deal done. Money was tight, but a hands-on owner was in charge and a workaholic coach who could handle duties off the field was at the helm. Jones declared he would make the organization "lean and mean," paring costs and many of the franchise's 100-plus employees.

The upside of the firestorm that began with Landry's firing was that the resulting pressure caused Jones to fight back by working overtime to prove every one of his vocal detractors wrong. Bounding about in his Lear and working out of the Airport Marriott hotel room he and wife Gene occupied for 40 days, Jones was working around the clock, as was Johnson, with their first minicamp approaching. Jones was sleeping in the office for four or five hours a night, dashing from meeting to meeting in a rumpled blue suit and well-worn blue button-down. His blue eyes were often stressed and bloodshot. The focus was on a single objective, the one thing Jones knew would earn respect of fans and fellow NFL owners—winning.

"We did not know what to do but roll up our sleeves and work," says Jones. "We had to find a way."

In his first half year on the job, he was criticized for breaking NFL protocol by publicly passing judgment on another team. He had said on the record in San Diego that the Chargers needed a quarterback, a rookie owner mistake. Jones apologized for the remark, but journalists learned that notepads and cameras should always be ready when he was around. Among other musings from Jones was his assessment that Cowboys employees before the franchise sale were underworked with 120 people doing the job that 30 people were doing at the Bengals franchise in Cincinnati. Staff members, he said, came to work at 9:30 AM, reading the paper, working out in the gym...waiting on game day. The players, he said, resented the staff's work ethic. All that would change,

35

he said. Jones went after the players, too, collectively at least. If they were not acting enthused, looking enthused, conducting themselves like they wanted to be Cowboys, he wanted them out.

Jones's outspoken manner was drawing headlines, but it was also working on behalf of his and the team's image. And it was not by accident, he says today. Some thought him to be a public-relations nightmare, but he was often calculated in his remarks. Sometimes the headlines came as a slip of the tongue, but usually he knew exactly what he was saying. Regardless of whether it was a faux paus or intentional, Skip Bayless, the columnist, noted that Jones does not back away from his remarks, even if he has to apologize for them. None of this "I did not know a reporter was in the room" stuff.

The style was uniquely Jerry Jones; part roughneck renegade Al Davis (owner of the Oakland Raiders), part expect-anything George Steinbrenner (owner of the New York Yankees), and part calculated showman Tex Schramm. Jones was learning that even if the media mentions were so-called negative, the headlines created fan intrigue. Thus, the Jones formula for raising the franchise from the dust was emerging: controversy + visibility = curiosity.

"It [the attention] is not all bad for the NFL," Jones was quoted as saying in 1989 in the *Dallas Times Herald.* "It's certainly not bad for the Cowboys. I think there are people who haven't watched NFL football much in Missouri or Ohio, and are aware *something* is going on with the Dallas Cowboys."

With its top pick in the 1989 draft, thanks to the Cowboys' last-place finish the previous season under Landry, Dallas chose UCLA quarterback Troy Aikman. Conventional wisdom had said all along that Dallas would take Aikman. Landry had his eye on the quarterback in his final months as coach, and UCLA had played Arkansas in the Cotton Bowl, a game Jerry Jones watched.

With blond hair, blue eyes, and a tall, prototypical quarterback frame, Aikman had the All-American look, the All-American build, and a franchise-building personality to provide payoff for Jones's big risk. The first-round draft choice would not come cheap, however, making some wonder if Dallas's new owner would part with the millions needed to get the deal done.

Aikman, who originally signed with Oklahoma and played one season for Barry Switzer in Stillwater before transferring to UCLA and becoming a West Coast star, knew Johnson because the Miami coach had recruited him twice; once out of high school and once after he left Oklahoma. The quarterback's agent, Leigh Steinberg, suggested publicly Aikman would not come on the cheap for the struggling Cowboys, and a longtime friend of Jones's suggested the new team owner watched every dollar as if it were his last, so big spending required to run a professional football team might be an issue. Jones did not disagree with the rumor, but countered, on his disregard for waste, "That doesn't mean there aren't times when you spend some money that doesn't necessarily make you a profit that day. What it means is that I can't live with waste."

Jones's strategy is to reduce expenses that do not directly impact having a successful team or business model. If flash makes a difference, buy it. If a player makes a difference, sign him. But if lights are burning with nobody in the room, turn them out.

Jones met for two consecutive days with Aikman and Steinberg, negotiating details in the back room of a popular Dallas restaurant. A waiter serving the group recalls word leaked out that the quarterback was in the restaurant and a group of young women congregated outside the room. While serving water to the table, he told Aikman about the group, but let him know he had told them it was just somebody who looked like the quarterback in the restaurant.

No, Aikman responded. Tell them it's me. Tell them I'll be out when we are finished.

After lunch, Aikman signed autographs for all to the delight of those gathered. Jones, the consummate promoter, knew he had his man. The deal was sealed as Jones turned heads throughout Dallas and the NFL when he successfully negotiated the Aikman contract at close to $11 million, an NFL record at the time for a first-round pick. Headlines, finally, were positive, but they would be among the last for Jones and the Cowboys for some time.

Any Given Sunday

"I don't sit around here and worry about getting voted out by a board of directors or anybody else. So my time is definitely not spent worrying over immediate results. My focus is what can be done in the way of making a contribution to our future success."

—Jerry Jones, after his team's winless start in 1989

3

Any Given Sunday

Jerry Jones did not arrive in the NFL as the shrinking violet type, waiting patiently for his given moment to reach full bloom. He stuck with the results-oriented, outspoken personality that had carried him thus far, possibly even adding a touch of flair for the high-profile stage offered by professional football and the Dallas Cowboys. The more intense the pressure and the bigger the issue, the more visible Jones became, grasping full responsibility for issues at hand with the greatest of force, no matter the consequences. Within his first year of ownership, Jones tackled old-guard owners in key decisions, challenged longstanding relationships without apology, and pulled off one of the most lopsided trades in the history of professional sports. Headline writers could hardly keep up.

Probably because the league was mired in mediocrity and needing change upon his arrival, the timing could not have been better for making an impact. Just after it was announced that Jones was buying the team, for instance, longtime commissioner Pete Rozelle announced his retirement. The popular choice for his replacement among older owners, including Mara, Modell, and Pittsburgh's Dan Rooney, was Jim Finks, formerly general manager of the New Orleans Saints. Finks was a football man. Jones and some of the league's newer owners did not feel he was a marketing man, however. NFL owners were scheduled to meet in Chicago during the summer, just weeks before Jones's first training camp, to vote on Finks, considered a shoo-in for the job.

Stormy weather and a radar glitch caused air traffic control problems, delaying flights, and many of the newer owners who did arrive, including Jones, gathered in an airport hotel bar, talking over drinks about the impending decision. Jones was one of the more vociferous of the 11 owners banding together in Chicago, letting his opinion be widely known that the NFL was a marketing gold mine with an established brand and a lucrative demographic. The more Jones and several other younger owners spoke, the more clear it became that Finks would not have the needed support to become commissioner. Four months would pass before league attorney Paul Tagliabue would be named Rozelle's successor, but the group, which became known as the "Chicago 11," had effectively shown the NFL's old guard that its new guard—Jones prominently included—had a voice to be reckoned with.

At home in Texas, Jones was having a rougher time. He fired the team's longtime public relations director along with literally a dozen or more key employees he felt were too loyal to the team's old ways of business. Public sentiment continued to run negative amid the fast, drastic changes, and rumors were rampant that Jones was in too deep financially. Local media was praising the purchase of Major League Baseball's Texas Rangers by a group including George W. Bush. That sale was said to have been handled right, while Jones was said to have bumbled through his purchase. Sophia Dembling, a special contributor in *The Dallas Morning News*, summed up the negative sentiment best in her open letter to the Cowboys' owner. "But you've got a way about you, Mr. Jones," she wrote. "It's very annoying. We realize you're a businessman, used to getting his way with no questions asked. But those days are over. You've got more people to answer to now than just your creditors. It seems every time you open your mouth, you say something wrong. And so loudly, too. Welcome to the fishbowl, Mr. Jones."

Behind the scenes, though, Jones and Johnson did not let the criticism slow them down. Every negative word and each doubting glare made them work harder. They lived at the office, analyzing the team's roster and player availability and seeking sponsors to help pay mounting bills. Texas Stadium had recently been remodeled, giving Jones more suites to sell for revenues, and he employed Johnson to help him make deals. Interested parties were invited to meet the owner and coach at the stadium. Jones made a pitch with an insurance salesman's flair and Johnson made the guests laugh.

"Jimmy was great," recalls Jones. "He really helped me out."

The franchise sold 28 of 33 new boxes available that year, generating $18 million. To give ticket holders more, Jones made changes off the field. He wanted the famous Dallas Cowboys Cheerleaders brought into modern times. Taking advice from Johnson, who thought the country music they performed was out of touch, Jones made rap and rock music a part of the cheerleaders' act. More than one dozen cheerleaders quit the squad in response to the modernizing move, making more news headlines, but they returned to work in three days and that was that.

Cheerleader problems were nothing compared with the other negative news mounting against Jones and the Cowboys, though. Jones was butting heads with Smith, the minority owner who tried to buy the team, over the team's financial stability, and Schramm and dozens of other former team employees were disgruntled and running to the media with every morsel of rumor, innuendo, and fact they could find. Some reports were true but exaggerated; others were not true at all. On Schramm's part, the backbiting was somewhat ironic since he and Jones had much in common, separated only by generation and style. Schramm talked about winning with class and style; Jones preferred winning, period, believing that success created class and style. Schramm of course was bitter over being let go and having to let Landry go, so he did not always hide his feelings when talking to journalists about Jones, making it clear that he didn't like the drastic changes the new owner was implementing. For his part, Jones liked Schramm and understood the reasons for his methods. He could not blame Schramm. The Cowboys had been his life.

Another concern was the team's ongoing financial despair. More than $29,000 a day was needed to run the franchise and the money was not there. Three times early into his ownership Jones had to dip into personal cash to pay bills. One media source reported Aikman's $1.5 million lump-sum signing bonus check was being held because the team did not have the money to pay it, but in fact it was ready on the day promised contractually. Jones would not allow for a slipup like that.

Jones was also said to have missed a $90,585 payment on the team's 30-acre Valley Ranch headquarters. In hindsight, he says he was overburdened with the lavish building. He tried to sell it to a physician group, but ultimately he restructured debt in accordance with Dallas's adjusted real estate market—at a 40 percent discount—which made him so proud of the building he began jokingly telling employees to "wipe their feet" before walking on the blue carpet.

The action that made the most impact in the early days by Jones, though, was undoubtedly his trade of running back Herschel Walker to the Minnesota Vikings, a move that set in motion the foundation of Cowboys teams of the 1990s, which would be known for one of the most dominating runs in the history of the NFL. Jones viewed Walker as an asset, but one he wanted to trade, not keep. Walker's contract was too expensive and his legs were tiring after so many carries. Using his salesmanship, Jones talked Vikings general manager Mike Lynn into a deal that would forever be stamped in NFL lore.

For one Herschel Walker and four later-round draft picks, Dallas got five players and many excellent early draft picks, including Minnesota's first- and second-round picks in 1990 (the Cowboys used the first pick in another trade to draft running back Emmitt Smith). In the end, Dallas got eight players almost immediately on its roster from the trade, including three starters. History would show the trade as a key moment in the league, but many Cowboys fans did not understand it at the time, considering Walker was viewed as one of the greatest running backs to ever play football. One person suggested Jones and Johnson were novices, learning on the fly.

That may have been true, but in getting rid of Walker, Jones was able to build a strong supporting cast for Aikman, his young new quarterback. The payoff, however, was down the road a bit. The trade further strained cash flow because Jones had to pay Walker $1.25 million in cash to accept the trade; this after he had paid Landry a $1 million severance as well as severance to dozens of other removed Cowboys employees. The trade hurt the team on the field, too, in the short term.

Dallas was outmanned during Jones's first season, losing its first nine games of the season. With a weak defense and no Herschel Walker to slow the game down, the team was awful. The Cowboys' lone win came on the road, a 13–3 victory at Washington.

The young Cowboys struggled, to say the least, seeking to avoid posting one of the worst seasons on record in the NFL. That is why Jones still recalls the solitary win that first season as among his best career victories as owner. The win over Washington was the game that taught him that on any given Sunday, any team can win. He keeps a souvenir signed game ball from the victory in his office, commemorating win number one. But as losses piled one onto another during the 1–15 season, so did criticisms. Smith, the minority owner, was unhappy. Schramm, the ex-employee, was unhappy. Fans who did not understand Jones's longer-term approach were unhappy.

To acknowledge feelings toward him and to make a point, Jones once walked into an employee meeting wearing a Darth Vader mask. Amid laughter, he took off the mask, showing he was not the evil character some made him out to be. But even the typically stoic Landry got into the criticizing act. Said Landry on ESPN, "The new ownership and the new coach came into an exciting situation for them. They didn't think about people. They thought about the opportunity they had. It's really a disappointment they don't rely on [the team's tradition]."

Every direction Jones turned, it seemed, trouble was brewing. Arkoma, the company he once owned with Mike McCoy, was under scrutiny and facing a class-action suit from shareholders of Arkla Inc. who argued McCoy and Jones improperly profited from the sale of their natural gas assets to the company. Jones and his partner ultimately had to reimburse shareholders money, but he says that was not as painful as the personal scrutiny he was under in regard to the Cowboys. Rumors were rampant and facts were blown way out of proportion. People were saying his marriage was in shambles and that he was broke. The *Dallas Times Herald* even ran a sensational headline in late November that year: "Last-Place Cowboys Having Trouble Paying Bills."

Two decades later, with family firmly intact and an annual spot on the *Forbes* list of the 400 richest Americans, Jones shakes his head, wondering how he survived, suffering only diagnosed heart arrhythmia and angst as a result. Looking back, he is still surprised how difficult the transition was but understands it was all part of the important shaping and learning process.

"I never did have a honeymoon," he says. "Never one night [because of the scrutiny that began with the Landry firing]. This was a period of time somebody brought $160 million to Texas at a time when everything was going down [including the football team]. We were suddenly quite visible. Some of it we asked for; some we didn't. You understood it came with the territory, but that did not make it easy. It really focused me, though. That kind of experience toughens you up."

During the team's on-field struggles, Jones assumed a position of positive visible profile. For every negative blow, he had an upbeat response. Reporters and columnists who ripped him received firm handshakes and broad smiles afterward. Frank Luksa, who poked at Jones many times in print in the *Dallas Times Herald*, remarked once that he expected to be written into Jones's will if he continued criticizing the owner, for, with each negative word, Jones became nicer and nicer and nicer. Columnist Skip Bayless concurred, writing: "The longer you criticize Jones, the harder he'll smile and pump your hand."

And even as the team was on its way to a franchise record in losses, Jones openly addressed the media and fans, explaining his processes each step along the way. Fans also got an early glimpse of Jones's unique, hands-on ownership style as he established that first season a habit and tradition of standing on the sideline during portions of many games. Unusual for NFL owners to be so near the action and in the line of fire of fans, he says he took to the field initially because he wanted to be a stand-up guy in the toughest of times. He wanted to show he could take the heat for firing Tom Landry and trading Herschel Walker. If fans did not like what he had done, they had an easy target for their frustrations.

They also got to see Jerry Jones was on their side. During an October game that first year he actually stepped onto the playing field to lecture a referee about a poor call. The Cowboys were playing San Francisco at Texas Stadium, a game they lost 31-14. In the final seconds of the game, Jones ran across the turf to berate the field judge. After the game, he complained about the officiating. Years later he realizes his intensity level was so high, emotions were often uncontrollable.

Jones never stopped going to the sideline, though, and his appearance near the Cowboys bench is traditional in his era the way Landry's hat was in Landry's era, whether people like it or not. Jones understands clearly the criticism that comes from some who think the owner should stay far away from the field, but he delivers a compelling argument in response. First of all, Jones says, he likes to go to the sideline during games because he can get a better "sense of the intensity level." Then, there is the support factor. He is more inclined to go down to the sideline from his perch in a personal luxury suite when the team is not playing well than when it is. But more is at stake than that.

"I have always been taken aback that people think an owner and general manager does not belong on the field," says Jones. "It is comparable to a manager of a manufacturing plant walking the floor to see the workers, to see the process. I'm not comfortable just sitting back. In any other business the owner or manager going to the floor would be perfectly natural. Just like when they [the Cowboys] score or make a big play, we are jumping up and down and hugging. I need that. I can't leave the emotion out. I don't want to."

The visibility, the positioning, and even the controversy were beginning to pay off for Jones and the Cowboys early in his tenure. Jones was learning that even if media attention is negative, it creates intrigue; in line with the old public relations adage, at least they are talking about you. He could see the dividends and did not plan on letting up. In 1990 Jones moved the team's training camp from California, where few fans attended practices, to Austin, Texas, drawing thousands. The move helped strengthen the brand in its home state and set a precedent for training camps that startled fellow NFL owners. Traditionally a costly venture—two decades ago teams spent $1 million or more for training camp—Jones made training camp a profit center while also building the team's fan base. He obtained sponsors, creating free events and practices for fans to attend.

47

"When I bought the Cowboys, I had to look for the meat and pota-toes," says Jones. "I had to put my hand on cold, hard assets because I had to put a lot of cash on the table to get this team."

Even though the Cowboys won just one game, the team sold more tickets and earned more revenue per fan in the stadium than the year before. The team's first exhibition game against San Diego was broad-cast on national television. ABC's *Primetime* news program ran a feature on Jones and the Cowboys. Things were changing and people were taking notice. Bayless, the columnist who along with Luksa had drilled the new owner repeatedly, eased up when asked by correspondent Judd Rose about laying into Jones in print.

"Look," Bayless said, "Dallas got sick of America's Team two years ago. But now I get the feeling people in this city are excited again."

All in the Family

Before Jerry Jones bought the Cowboys, the team was known as a fam-ily unit of sorts because so many employees, from Landry to Schramm to Brandt, had worked together for so many years. Jones, however, gave new definition to football family when the franchise became his. Gene, his wife, has been involved behind the scenes from the start, contrib-uting management advice, hosting special guests, and making sugges-tions for a new stadium. Stephen, the Joneses' oldest son, is CEO of the franchise, running the team on a day-to-day basis. Charlotte Jones Anderson, the Joneses' daughter, was valedictorian at Little Rock High School and a Stanford graduate (human biology and organizational management) who worked in Washington, D.C., before taking over as the franchise's executive vice president of brand management and special events. Jerry Jr. is executive vice president and chief sales and marketing officer.

The Joneses' family involvement often catches those who only see the game-day face of the Cowboys off guard. Jerry Jones and the team's head coach are the most visible publicly outside of players, but behind the scenes the family is exceptionally and unusually involved in fran-chise operations. Beginning with that first season, Gene has not missed a single game since the family has owned the team. Not one. She's interested in the inner workings of the team and knows background on players. At the team's first training camp in Austin, Jones recalls that when a big storm blew up before a team picnic, Gene was running with Charlotte, table to table, gathering up cloths blowing away in the high winds. Since her husband is "so uptight" on game days, she plays host to the family's special guests, ranging over the years from Mexico's former president Vicente Fox to former U.S. presidential candidate Ross Perot to freedom fighter Nelson Mandela. Jones watches most games from a small suite in the end zone at Texas Stadium, which has television monitors and enough room for him and his sons, but no more, by design.

Jones involved his children the way his father involved him in the family business. He was made an executive vice president right out of college, and each of his children has been given considerable authority as well. Besides running the franchise operationally, Stephen negotiates player contracts, and while Jerry always signs off on them, the deal is often "99 percent done" by the time it reaches his desk. Jerry Jr. has responsibility over franchise sponsorship opportunities, with training camp being one example. With an office that connects to his father's, he often slides in mornings for catch-up visits, talking about family and business opportunities the way co-workers might.

"All three are compromised because of their relationship with me," says Jones. "They recognize how we got here. I'm very sensitive about being a bully, because I can be. For me, though, it is opposite of what you hear about, the parent being too hard on his children at the office. They are allowed to do things I might not tolerate from somebody else. But they also give us value we would not have otherwise.

"I look at it with Gene, Stephen, Charlotte, myself, and Jerry Jr., as we have five heads. When we travel together or spend holidays together it is like having a board meeting. Everybody has input."

One just has to take their word, but suggestions from all say family holidays and vacations often turn into one big executive retreat, with every aspect of the Cowboys on the table for debate. But it was Charlotte who got the difficult duty of calling Tom Landry in 1990 to see if the former coach would graciously accept induction into the team's Ring of

Honor with Bob Lilly and Roger Staubach. Tall, attractive, and personable, Charlotte is known for having her father's drive and her mother's charm. She also displays a passion, a kind of you-can't-turn-me-down infectiousness, the same type of convincing irresistibility her father displays. When the Cowboys score, she high-fives her father if he's in the vicinity, and when they lose she takes it as hard as he and other family members do. The invitation to Landry, then, would have seemed to be a sure thing in regard to his acceptance, but it did not work out that way. Polite but terse, Landry declined the first offer.

No thank you, he said.

Jones was dismayed, even if he had gone about firing Landry the wrong way. Coaching was a business of hiring and firing. Everybody in football knew that. The opportunity to join the Ring of Honor was an olive branch, a well-deserved peace offering. The franchise could do nothing about it but offer, though, so Jones moved on for the time being, focusing on getting the team out of the red financially and out of the NFL's cellar record-wise. With the team's financial prospects on the rise and a season of turmoil behind him, Jones moved successfully to remove limited partner Ed Smith from ownership through buyout. Within a year, he had taken most other minority owners out as well, giving him 95 percent control of the Dallas Cowboys and 100 percent control of Texas Stadium. Searching for more revenue streams, he asked the City of Irving, which controlled licensing for the stadium, to allow beer sales at games. The request set off another controversy, placing Jones at the center.

Long before Jones owned the team, Texas Stadium employed a brown-bag alcohol policy. Anything fans wanted to bring into the game themselves was allowed. Fans toted ice chests containing dozens of beers and bags containing fifths of liquor through the turnstiles, turning contests into miniature unmanaged alcohol festivals. Jones and the franchise had no service control and no revenue, a losing proposition for such a business. Imagine baseball's Wrigley Field or New Orleans's Superdome with no beer sales. Jones recalls stadium cleanup crews were collecting literally 10,000 discarded liquor bottles and 80,000 discarded beer cans from the stands after big games. But

Jerry Jones asking for beer rights in Texas Stadium did not go over well. He and Gene attended a city council meeting, sitting in the audience for hours late into the night as church members and citizens complained, suggesting Tom Landry would never do such a thing. It was not easy, but Jones pleaded his case, ultimately getting a beer license for the stadium. Other challenges as the Dallas owner were beginning to go his way as well.

In moving the team's training camp to Austin, Jones became the first NFL owner to actually profit from practice, getting sponsors for golf and black-tie events and dominating the local news in the heart of Texas, making the Lone Star State a Cowboys state as more than 100,000 fans attended. He got a letter from President George II.W. Bush, addressed to "Jerold W. Jones, coach of the Cowboys," thanking him for the gift of a replica helmet and jersey and providing well wishes. Jones made a joke of the coaching reference, saying, "If the president says it's so...." And Jones bought out one of the team's last minority owners, taking complete and full control of the team, a position he relished as franchise fortunes were moving in the right direction. Gambles and hard work were paying off and he began to see that his large, risky investment might work.

"You'll do all right in business if you are right 50 percent of the time," he said in 1990.

The way things were developing, he was 100 percent right in buying the Dallas Cowboys. Jones became the first NFL owner to host his own TV show and write a regular column for the daily newspaper. He was also a regular on the radio airwaves after the Cowboys negotiated a new broadcast rights contract with station KVIL for $4 million, double what was paid by the previous station, KRLD. Jones involved Johnson in the negotiations, rare for a coach, but Jones crossed over in duties for an owner as well, attending practices, sitting in on strategy and personnel meetings, and staying abreast of game plans. Johnson was named NFL Coach of the Year by the Associated Press following the 1990 season when the Cowboys posted a 7–9 record, narrowly missing the playoffs. The results were quite a turnaround from the one-win season of Jones and Johnson just a year before.

In 1991, Dallas won its final five games of the regular season to cap an 11-win year, the team's best since 1983. The Cowboys beat the eventual Super Bowl champion Washington Redskins on the road in late November and won a first-round playoff game on the road at Chicago 17–13. Emmitt Smith and Michael Irvin became the first two players from the same team to lead the NFL in rushing yardage and receiving yardage in the same season. The franchise was back and on its way to returning to the Super Bowl. It was also regaining its distinction as America's Team as Smith had 1,563 yards rushing and Irvin set single-season club records for receptions (93) and receiving yardage (1,523). Both players were named to the NFC Pro Bowl. The team finished the season with the fifth-highest ticket price and drew on average 62,737 fans per game that season, compared to just 49,141 during Landry's last season. Combined with the fact that Dallas had the NFL's fifth-lowest payroll—Jones released aging veteran defensive back Everson Walls, for instance, in part because of his $600,000 salary—the owner was looking as if he could manage the team after all.

Wrote Frank Luksa in the *Dallas Times Herald*: "He [Jones] can sell. He can sell shoelaces for house shoes. Everything he owns is for sale. His ability to peddle for profit is a source of wonder."

But as the media began to shower praise on the owner, the team's coach became more silent and distant in regard to Jones. Johnson apparently did not want Jones getting credit for the team's turnaround, insinuating at many opportunities that the owner was a lightweight in professional football. Johnson took credit for the Walker trade, yet it was Jones who wrote the check for $1 million to get the running back to take the trade and move to Minnesota. Both the owner and the coach worked the media at every opportunity, but the acts were individual. For instance, before an NFC playoff game against Detroit in 1991—a game the Cowboys lost—Jones told a journalist that injured quarterback Troy Aikman was secure in his job, unthreatened by Cowboys backup Steve Beuerlein. When Johnson read the owner's remarks in the paper, he was incensed.

"Who is running the football team?" he roared. "Is Jerry the coach or am I the coach? To hell with it! If I'm not running things, maybe I should take my whole staff and we'll move to Tampa Bay!"

Regardless of the employee backbiting, Jones's enthusiasm with winning was significant and obvious to the point that he admitted having to contain his "over-enthusiasm." But he was making in-roads at almost every corner in his role as Dallas Cowboys owner and general manager. Among league owners, Jones cast the deciding vote to keep instant replay in games, and he joined Kansas City owner Lamar Hunt in openly fighting the league's discussed realignment, effectively suggesting that tradition was one of the NFL's most treasured and valuable assets. And by parlaying the Walker trade into timely draft choices and paying more than $1 million in signing bonuses to help the team land 16 Plan B free agents, Jones ensured Dallas's talent level was vastly improved. The once-downtrodden namesake city was afire with Cowboys fever in a mere two years. Talk about a turnaround.

Also, by micromanaging every aspect of the team's off-field opportunities and exposure, Jones was opening previously closed doors. The best example might be when Jones, dismayed because the Cowboys were not on CBS for every regular-season game in Little Rock, his former hometown, called the KTHV television station general manager at home, finding his unlisted telephone number through connections.

People there care about the Dallas Cowboys, Jones said.

This is a big story in Arkansas, he continued.

They feel like it is their team, too, Jones said.

So why don't you call the network and see if they will let you show the Cowboys every week? Jones strongly suggested.

One quality of Jerry Jones people quickly learn when getting to know him is that when he gets his mind set on something, something he is convinced is in the best interest of all parties at hand, saying no becomes a challenge. Thus, the phone call to the network was made and the Dallas Cowboys became Arkansas's team, gaining an unusually high 55 percent market share.

Controversy, however, was not past tense in Irving. Jones fired longtime director of player personnel Bob Ackles, replacing him with his 27-year-old son, Stephen. The transfer happened rather bizarrely at Dallas's Valley Ranch headquarters one Thursday afternoon in 1992. As Ackles was leaving the offices following his termination meeting with Jones, the agent of defensive tackle Chad Hennings arrived for a meeting. Stephen Jones—not Ackles, already relieved of his duties and headed out the door—met with Hennings's agent. A former college player possessing a degree in chemical engineering, Stephen is known for his intellect, likability, and being quite different from his father. Never seeking the limelight, Stephen is a business pragmatist willing to make tough decisions, yet he often uses a more patient, diplomatic approach, making him a good business match for Jerry Jones. On his first day in the office with added responsibilities, he did not let age or inexperience stand in the way, telling Hennings's agent the tackle's contract would not be renegotiated.

Sorry.

Ackles went on to join the Phoenix Cardinals' staff while Stephen became one of the league's youngest executives, ultimately rising to CEO of the Dallas Cowboys. Some at the time may have considered the move a bit unusual, but Jones considered it good business. Nobody, after all, would watch the Cowboys' money like his son, who also happened to be quite qualified.

Said Jones, "If Bob came to me and said, 'Just 20K more and we have a deal [with a player],' I might hesitate. But if Stephen says the same thing, I'm more comfortable because it's Stephen's money, too."

A Super-Sized Payoff

"We have operated in a
fearless manner. I've been
asked, 'Did you have a
five-year program?' I had
no program. All I thought
was we had to do it as
quickly as we could without
damaging the long term. Be
as aggressive as we could.
Do it yesterday."

–Jerry Jones

4

A Super-Sized Payoff

Being right is the ultimate vindication in controversy and nobody enjoys the position more than Jerry Jones. Hoisting a Super Bowl trophy high in the air after just three topsy-turvy years as owner of the Dallas Cowboys was gratification for the owner, and then some. For all the grief endured over every struggle incurred from the moment he fired Tom Landry to trying to get a beer license in Irving for Texas Stadium, Jones got professional football's ultimate award more quickly than anyone could have imagined. The fact that the Dallas Cowboys made such a quick turnaround—from a one-win season in 1989 to winning the Super Bowl three years later—is difficult to grasp so many years later. That is why the turnaround will go down as one of the greatest role reversals in American sports history.

Like its once-failing economy, Dallas was a franchise in disarray in the late 1980s, and the many changes instituted by Jones came so hard and fast that observers probably did not know whether they were for the good or bad. Jones wondered himself in quiet moments, fearing that if the team did not win quickly his harshest critics would get a firm hold. The payoff for Jones and the Cowboys came soon, though, as the team, like Dallas's economy, made a hard and fast comeback, providing dramatic testimony that both the owner and the franchise were once again forces to be reckoned with in the NFL. No longer an outsider and no longer a cellar dweller, Jones and Dallas were firmly in the loop and on top of the league when they blitzed through the regular season in 1992. With 13 wins earned behind the offensive prowess of Aikman, Irvin, and Smith, the timely and effective field leadership of Jimmy Johnson, and aided by an underrated defense, Dallas won the NFC title 30–20 on the road at then–perennial power San Francisco and mauled Buffalo 52–17 in Super Bowl XXVII before 133 million viewers, making it the most watched television event in history at the time.

The season was a Cinderella story, the type sporting dreams are made of as the former underdogs, led by a strong-armed, poster-boy quarterback and a big-smile, quick-cutting running back, turned aggressive, taking down opponents with the authority of seasoned champions. For Jones, the 1992 season was the quietest in his short tenure as owner and general manager as media focus was on the players and results from the playing field for a change. Stories were still unfolding behind the scenes, though, just without as much fanfare and controversy. Someone from the Cowboys had followed up on Charlotte's first call to Landry, but the coach continued to avoid accepting induction into the franchise's Ring of Honor.

My schedule won't allow, Landry said.

The NFL was also looking into Dallas's "quick signing" of players after the spring draft, accusing Jones of making deals to secure picks before they were officially chosen. Also, franchise foundation wide receiver Michael Irvin held out before the start of the season, testing Jones to see whether he would raise his final $3.75 million per year offer, but Jones did not easily budge.

"This is what the job pays," said Jones. "Michael needs to know that. It's already reached the point where I'm uncomfortable. But we're willing to show the confidence we have in him by going this far. He needs to know how serious I am. This is what the job pays."

Irvin countered, "I want Jerry to know how serious I am about my numbers, too. This drawing-the-line business isn't negotiating."

Jones got Irvin back in uniform with a contract each was happy with, and the wide receiver played a critical role in the Cowboys' run to three Super Bowl wins in the 1990s. The former University of Miami receiver would ultimately find off-field trouble, however, facing a felony drug possession charge and other battles in his Dallas career before landing in the Pro Football Hall of Fame. On the field, though, Irvin was spectacular during the 1992 season, a main reason Dallas was ripping through opponents behind offensive strength and defensive balance. With Smith, they could run. With Irvin, they could throw. With Aikman, the Cowboys could do both with relative ease.

Dallas kicked its season off with an international preseason game, planned by a young NFL executive director named Roger Goodell, and introduced in the regular season with a live postgame TV and radio show designed to show the spontaneity and candor of the locker room. The 40-minute program was a first in the NFL; no longer would fans be relegated to locker-room stories as reported briefly in the next day's newspaper. The season unfolded without a hitch as the team drew sellouts for each of its eight home games, climbing atop the NFC East.

But late in the year, despite being on the cusp of a franchise-best regular season, Johnson was criticized by fans following a 20–17 loss on the road to Washington when the team fumbled in the end zone near the end, letting victory slip away, and he did not take it well. Johnson barely talked about the game with the media afterward, and he had tense words with an assistant coach and several players on the team flight back to Texas. Jones had been encouraging Johnson to raise more hell on the sideline like former Chicago Bears head coach Mike Ditka, but he was not pleased with how Johnson handled losing during a season that was so otherwise promising. For the first time, people closely watching the program began to ask what was wrong with "J and J," Jones and Johnson. Tension was obviously growing between the two, and although the team won big, the coach was showing stress from the job. Jones was asked about it and, as he always does, he gave an answer.

"Where I sit, I cannot tell people to kiss my ass," Jones said. "Where Jimmy sits, he feels he can. For the first time in his coaching career, he doesn't have to recruit and he doesn't have to deal with alumni."

In other words, Johnson did not feel he had to answer to anybody. This was increasingly a problem for Jones, Johnson's boss, who enjoys the benefits of mild controversy surrounding the team because headlines keep fans interested. He arrived in the league as the most accessible owner and general manager, and he expected his coaches to provide the same benefits-driven accessibility. Johnson, however, did not want to answer to anybody if he did not want to, including Jones. The Cowboys were marching toward a historic season, but the coach and owner were having their first significant and publicly detected communication problem. Onlookers were beginning to realize the onetime college roommates were not as close as previously believed. Jones was determined to be the most involved owner in the history of the game, managing personnel and making draft picks, and he expected the coach to be on the same page.

"I paid a great deal for the Cowboys and the stadium," said Jones. "It was my own money, not a [big] consortium. That's a real good way to get committed."

Johnson, however, wanted to be Tom Landry and Tex Schramm combined, and he wanted Jones to be Clint Murchison Jr., the owner completely out of his business.

"Winning changed Jimmy," says Jones.

Johnson did not seem to mind Jones when the team was losing and the owner was getting clobbered in the press, but a power struggle ensued after the Cowboys started winning. Increasing strain between the two did not stop Jones from enjoying the wild winning road to the top. As the 1992 season wore on, he could sense this was a team of destiny, one benefiting from player talent and chemistry and the right bounce of the ball—shades of his college team from 1964.

Typically Jones was on the field before the game and again sometime in the fourth quarter. But during the team's first playoff game at home against Philadelphia that year, Jones was bounding all over the stadium, high-fiving Hank Williams Jr., who was in attendance, and getting the crowd excited with fist pumps, thumbs-up signals, and big smiles.

"In all candor, I just could not stay off the field," said Jones.

Enthusiasm was hard for Jones to contain at the Super Bowl, an event custom-made for the showman aspect of his personality. When sitting for an interview with *The Washington Post* the week before the big game, Jones joked that upon first meeting Jack Kent Cooke, who then owned the Redskins, he "could not visit long because he needed to get to the field to tell Jimmy Johnson what plays to call in the fourth quarter."

To reach the game and festivities, held in California, he chartered a jet from Little Rock and flew 160 close friends and guests out for wining, dining, football, and a final, no-expense-spared celebration at the Santa Monica Civic Center. The invitation was one nobody could turn down without a good excuse—except for Tom Landry. Jones had someone with the Cowboys contact Landry, talking with the former coach's coordinators about attending the Super Bowl as a Cowboys guest—the franchise's first trip to the sport's ultimate game without Landry.

"Our communication with his people has indicated to me that his schedule just wouldn't permit," said Jones. "I know that Tex [Schramm] was coming and I knew Coach Landry would be out here, but I have not had any thoughts about [inviting him]. Our communication with his people has indicated to me that his schedule wouldn't permit it. That's the way it's been on any of the things we've talked about, especially the Ring of Honor. I had no reason to believe this would be any different."

Using the Super Bowl as vindication for three years of hard work and suffering, Jones did not miss a single Super Bowl event and was often the first to arrive and the last to leave. At the traditional Super Bowl media press conference, he manned his very own microphone. Never before in the 26 years the NFL had hosted a Super Bowl press conference had an owner manned a microphone alongside the head coach and star players, yet here was Jones, holding proverbial court for journalists from around the world. Jones points out that an owner having a microphone today is commonplace. But on that day, at that time, he was the first and nobody was sure what to make of it. Naturally, Jones did not exactly handle himself in the limelight with pursed lips either. He started talking and continued for 90 minutes, some 30 minutes longer than league officials had scheduled.

That is the thing about Jones. Some people may think he talks incessantly about football because he loves to hear himself talk, but as that day illustrates, he talks about football incessantly because he loves talking about football. Spend time with him away from the field or when he is around friends or family and you will find that Jones can be soft-spoken and a good listener. But get him talking about the Dallas Cowboys and the future of the NFL or football in general and be ready for one opinion followed by another. Journalists love this, of course. Jones has long been a media darling once the Dallas columnists stopped taking their weekly swings at him. They figured out he could be a great sound bite or the subject of an award-winning column. Journalists are always looking for quotes, and coaches are too often guarded because they have owners and general managers watching and listening to every word. Jones does not fear losing his job because he has no boss, so he is known to tell it like it is, for better or worse. Some were initially surprised at that first Super Bowl press conference that Jones manned a microphone and talked until his pigskin-warmed heart was content, but he says the owner and general manager of a professional team should naturally be involved in the Super Bowl, particularly when they are one in the same.

Cowboys head coach Jimmy Johnson was not exactly comfortable with sharing the stage with the team owner, but as 90 minutes of smiles, insight, and football colloquialisms proved, Jerry Jones was quite comfortable. So much so that he stayed in the media room for several hours afterward, talking with journalists until past 9:00 PM that night, an evening on which he was taking Gene out to celebrate their 30th wedding anniversary at a nearby restaurant. She understood his tardiness, of course, because she shared in the enthusiasm.

The Dallas Cowboys were in the Super Bowl!

Just three years before, they were on their knees, and Jerry and Gene Jones were privately wondering what they had gotten themselves into. So they had a grand old time in California, as anyone would expect. Gene was honored with breakfast at Tiffany's. Jerry was toasted by the governor of California and interviewed on network morning shows. None of it trumped the clinchers, though, which occurred in the aftermath of Dallas destroying the Bills. Jones clutched the winning trophy in his right hand following the presentation ceremony and, with his left arm clutched around the neck of Jimmy Johnson, he hoisted the trophy high, pumping his left fist while smiling ever so broadly.

Hours later, after players had cleared from the locker room and television cameras were turned off, Jones was lifted by helicopter from the Rose Bowl in Pasadena where his team had just dismantled Buffalo. The moment gave great pause to his years-long professional journey.

"I thought, *How could I have ever dreamed it?*" Jones said. "Lifting out of the Rose Bowl after winning the Super Bowl? It was almost surreal."

Two months later, Jones took his Dallas Cowboys to Washington to be honored at the White House by President Bill Clinton, an Arkansas native. Around the same time, Jones handed out the team's Super Bowl rings, valued at $13,000 each. The NFL had contributed roughly $4,400 to the pot, but Jones did not want his championship players to have anything less than the best to commemorate the win, so he kicked up the ante. This for the owner was no wasteful electric bill but rather a well-earned reward for achieving the ultimate: a Super Bowl victory.

Leveling the Playing Field

Sports commentary is often little more than worn-out, repeated clichés, but one phrase that never becomes old or untrue for Jones is the one about winning being a cure for all ills. In Dallas and in the eyes of many journalists and fans, winning the Super Bowl helped transform the Cowboys' owner and general manager from a thrillbilly into someone who is not only serious about the football business but also pretty good at it, too. Winning the Super Bowl turned many his way, including Tom Landry. The retired Hall of Fame coach had turned down the multiple invitations to join Dallas's Ring of Honor, and he had declined to be among the team's special guests at the Super Bowl. But not long after the team won the championship, Landry finally agreed to join them.

Yes, maybe a spot in Dallas's famed Ring of Honor was not such a bad idea after all.

Jones had met with Landry at a summer golf tournament. They had not spoken in the four years since Jones fired him. Jones did not regret doing it, certainly not with results in hand, but he did wish it had gone better, differently. So Jones went out of his way at the summer golf tournament to make amends, and it worked. Flanked by Jones and smiling accordingly with adulating applause, Landry was inducted into the Cowboys' Ring of Honor on November 7, 1993, officially closing the book on his firing controversy.

Victories were quickly piling up for Jones in many areas surrounding the team and the league. Recall him joining the Chicago 11 in overruling older, traditional NFL owners to name Tagliabue commissioner over Finks. Jones's primary reason in actively supporting this move was getting a commissioner who understood the value of television, since television was the primary source of income for franchises through the league's system of distributed revenue sharing. Jones had experience in television, as he once owned a small affiliate station in Arkansas, and he had done his homework before buying the Cowboys, visiting with Dan Burke of ABC in New York and asking dozens of questions about the relationship between networks and the league.

Burke had convinced Jones that the NFL had America's best reality show long before reality shows came into vogue. With games played once a week on a day when viewers are more apt to be at home watching television, interest-grabbing NFL storylines had one full week to unfold in the media. Major League Baseball has games every day and beat journalists can hardly keep up. The same story is told in regard to the National Basketball Association: a big Saturday home game can hardly get due coverage with the team on the road for a Wednesday contest.

Jones says this homework helped him to understand that professional football is not too dissimilar from professional wrestling, except that in football, games are 100 percent unscripted and real. Wrestling companies such as the WWE, led by Vince McMahon, learned in the 1980s that fans respond with passion to scripting, setting of the plot, and flash and circumstance. Therefore, through study, Jones set out in his strategy of building the Cowboys and the NFL to mimic the showmanship of professional wrestling, with rock music, gyrating cheerleaders, and cameras up close and personal to the action, while protecting the game's integrity by keeping it completely real. The payoff when you get it all right is must-see television, the ultimate entertainment and sporting medium.

When Jones joined the league, discussions were under way with owners to lower the value of the broadcast rights contract. The NFL had benefited for many years from lucrative contracts, but television executives argued they were losing money, successfully convincing many longtime league owners they would have to actually reduce fees to keep the networks and NFL exposure viable. Jones never bought into the argument, recalling a story from his days as a TV station owner. Jones was "getting clobbered" by a Little Rock competitor in the 1970s who used *I Love Lucy* reruns to launch into evening programming. Jones knew how costly reruns of the popular show were and could not imagine the other station made money on them. Curiosity got the best of Jones, and one day he talked with his competitor about the strategy, receiving a valuable lesson in entertainment economics. *I Love Lucy* reruns cost more than the station could earn in revenue for its allocated 30-minute time slot, but the popular show attracted viewers, launching them into other programs such as the locally produced evening news and following prime-time network shows. By losing money on the reruns, the competitive station was actually making more money, justifying the costly syndication expense.

"A loss leader," says Jones, "is worth something if it makes everything else worth more."

It is interesting to note that Jones helped shape the future of the NFL by closely listening to another; while his public persona usually depicts him as a talker, the Cowboys owner and general manager has a history of going, seeing, listening, and learning before making decisions. Drop by his office one day and Jeffrey Immelt, chairman and CEO of General Electric, is there, on a mission to learn about a new stadium under construction in Dallas, but Jones is the one who typically asks more questions in such meetings. Seek Jones at a Cowboys closed walk-through practice the day before the Cowboys play a game on NBC's *Sunday Night Football* and expect to find him standing next to Dick Ebersol, the noted television producer and executive who serves as chairman of NBC Sports, asking question after question. He works at knowing and usually, as a result, knows.

Through experience and questioning, Jones knew, for example, that the NFL was worth far more than the networks were saying in trying to convince owners to take a reduced contract. Jones ably convinced enough fellow NFL owners to see the light. The league was a gold mine for networks, bringing together millions of viewers in a key purchasing demographic at the most opportune time of the entire year, the prime-time fall season and the holidays. Because of Jones's timely leadership, the NFL signed a new television contract that increased revenue per team from the $17 million each received in 1989, the year he bought the Cowboys, to $38 million per team in 1993. The contract was historic. CBS, which long controlled NFL broadcast rights for Sunday games, had underestimated their value and Fox took it all away, stealing NFC games, which included some of the most desirable markets such as New York, Dallas, Chicago, and Philadelphia, in a $1.58 billion deal. The sudden hike in broadcast fees would help change the long-term fortunes of the league, generating more money than many owners ever conceived possible. The additional television revenue, combined with his team's on-field success, gave Jones a vision that his purchase of the Dallas Cowboys would not result in a dry hole. Gold was in that football team and the strike felt better than any time he authorized drilling deep into the earth and came up wealthy.

"In 36 months I saw I was going to be able to pay for it," he says. "The television upturn, the team's improvement, all began to hit about the third year. You could see it all coming together."

For the NFL, the moment of the new television deal was historic; for Jerry Jones, the moment was transforming. By showing fellow owners and league officials that the NFL commands the most American sports fans with the most buying power, he was able to convince them that the brand's worth in terms of television contracts and licensing was considerably more than anyone had ever known before. It was a new way of looking at professional football as not just a game of four quarters confined to a field and a stadium; it is a platform for launching multiple growth brand opportunities. The sport is so much bigger than the game. Thus, Jones's leadership was not only changing the fortunes of the Dallas Cowboys, but also positioning the NFL to emerge in the 21st century as one of the most successful business models in the world. Coming in the same year that Jones won the Super Bowl and was named by the NFL to its Competition Committee, becoming the first owner since the late Paul Brown to serve in that capacity, the Dallas owner seemed to have it all.

But the NFL has a way of bringing even the most upbeat back to reality. Hypercompetitiveness is a way of life in the league. Score and the other team has an answer; win, and a loss is just around the corner. Rise from the cellar and your players want more money and the other teams want your available players and assistant coaches. Therefore, for Jones and the Cowboys, prosperity was taking a toll as the 1993 season rolled around. Emmitt Smith, who helped the Cowboys win the Super Bowl, was a holdout at the beginning of the season. Without him in the backfield, the Cowboys lost the first two games, on the road at Washington (35–16) and at home to Buffalo (13–10). Fans watched closely, wondering whether Jones would blink. He did, for good reasons, signing the popular and prolific running back to a four-year contract worth more than $13 million including $7 million in up-front cash. Jones had been arguing in public that Smith's agent wanted "quarterback" or "Reggie White" money, but ultimately he needed Smith in the backfield and avoided salary cap issues down the road by providing much of the money as a one-time signing bonus.

The move was wise, considering Smith helped the Cowboys win 12 of the next 14 regular-season games upon his return, rushing for 1,486 yards and winning a third-straight NFL rushing crown. The dynasty at that point was well under way in Dallas. The Cowboys were emerging as the Team of the 1990s, piecing together a run that was previously unequaled in the league.

By the time the Cowboys won a second consecutive Super Bowl following the 1993 season, defeating Buffalo 30–13 at the Georgia Dome in Atlanta, Jones was meeting for more than an hour and a half in a hotel room with Luksa, the columnist, thinking out loud about his relationship with Johnson, the man who had replaced Landry and signed a 10-year contract. With his words, Jones was saying everything was all right in the fifth year of the owner/coach relationship, but at the same time he was wondering whether everything really was okay. Almost concurrently, Johnson was telling a member of the media he would be interested in the available head coaching job of the NFL's Jacksonville Jaguars expansion team, a remark obviously meant to publicly jab at Jones. Never mind that Johnson was one of the highest-paid coaches in the league and was under contract until 1998.

After hearing Johnson's comment, Jones said he was sure the coach was joking, but it was obvious the owner and coach were involved in a testy chess match power struggle and this was Johnson's way of making a move for checkmate.

And it worked!

Jones enjoyed his second consecutive Super Bowl to the fullest extent possible under the circumstances, bounding as he had the year before from event to event without sign of fatigue. One scribe noted the spotlight certainly agreed with Jones as he glided from one interview to the next, talking about how the organization was fueled by his "energy and enthusiasm" and that in all of his years in business he had never, ever worked harder. But he says in hindsight the conflict with Johnson had begun to wear on him. In previous key business relationships he was used to more of a backslapping working camaraderie where each helped the other, but as the team's owner, he felt the team's coach was no longer on his side. Thus, Jimmy Johnson's second Super Bowl victory with Dallas would be his last. The ending of Jones and Johnson made headlines around the country, but the story was as big in Dallas as the day Landry was fired. *The Dallas Morning News* listed it as the number one story in the metro area of 1994, leaving the owner to explain, years later, how and why.

"Jimmy has so many good qualities," said Jones, reflecting on the former Cowboys coach in his Valley Ranch office 13 years after Johnson's departure. "Our time together was rewarding. He was just a tough guy [for me] to be married to."

The Owner's Prerogative

"Only in an enterprise as narcissistic as professional football could a man be accused of 'meddling' in his own business."

—*Author Gary Cartwright*
on Jerry Jones

5

The Owner's Prerogative

Dallas Cowboys fans in particular and professional football fans in general will probably always ask the question in regards to Jerry Jones and Jimmy Johnson, who seemed to have a golden touch together in football that led the franchise to unprecedented business growth and two Super Bowl victories. Why couldn't they make the relationship work longer than five years?

To understand, one has to look at how it unraveled and why, assessing whether the association would have worked into the future under any circumstances. Winning, of course, has long posed problems in all levels of sports, but particularly so in the high-dollar, high-ego game of professional sports like the NFL. Dynasties simply do not last forever, and from the time Johnson arrived in 1989 until he left after the 1993 season, the Cowboys had a run that, at the time, was unequaled in the NFL. Dallas went in the matter of a few short years from woefully ineffective to unequaled elite, and such dramatic turnarounds always have a price.

For the Cowboys, that primary price of winning was considerable stress between the franchise's two biggest personalities, Jones and Johnson. Reflecting on the situation years later, Jones talks about the breakup as if he will never forget the smallest details, understanding well the scrutiny it will always be under. Jones has a long list of reasons the owner/coach partnership no longer worked, some attributable to Johnson and some attributable to himself. "He's got a long list on me, too," Jones says.

But the instigating factor, he says, was winning, which changed dynamics so that the association no longer worked. In the early days, Jones's and Johnson's desire to be the best drove them to a synergistic relationship that helped overcome personality conflicts. At Arkansas, they were friends with a singular goal: helping the Razorbacks win. Broyles was the coach and he got the credit. Off the field, however, the two men could not be more different outside of a shared competitive fire to be the best. Jones was a family man, a hugger and backslapper who enjoyed big gatherings and up-close-and-personal warmth. Johnson was more of an individual, divorced with strained personal relationships. Johnson preferred holidays on a boat in waters off the Miami coastline as opposed to dinner with 50 people in Dallas.

The relationship worked in the beginning because Jones and Johnson were driven to find a way, together, to reach the top and silence their critics. They worked around the clock, blending personality and wit with sheer work ethic. From a sports perspective, Jones and Johnson were Desi Arnaz and Lucille Ball or Dean Martin and Jerry Lewis, the consummate, never-a-dull-moment partners that fed off one another. Anybody paying close attention, though, could see the professional relationship would not last forever—or even more than five years.

Beginning in 1989, Jones and Johnson had spent endless hours together courting team sponsors, wining and dining patrons with charm based on old football stories and a gentleman's warming wit, and seeking every possible competitive advantage they could find for the team, from cheerleader routine changes to franchise-altering trades. Jones and Johnson hosted other owners and coaches in Jones's suite at NFL owners meetings for drinks and lively conversation, and Jones encouraged the coach to be a significant face and voice of the organization. They had conflicts in the early days but were able to resolve them, with Jones having final authority as owner and general manager and Johnson submitting, as employees are required to do. But jealousies and frustrations became exponentially larger as one big win piled onto another. Jones felt Johnson was undermining and no longer supportive. Johnson felt Jones clung too tightly to his ownership powers, refusing to give the coach control beyond game-day decisions. None of the conflict was uncommon in the professional sporting world. Recall only that Landry would barely talk to Bright years before because he felt the owner was too critical. So when asked about the relationship and conflict with Johnson, Jones was pointed in response.

"We've had issues, but not debates," he said. "We make the call."

Communication, however, became more strained between Jones and Johnson after the second Super Bowl victory. Jones began to lose his patience considering the team was his and he wanted—demanded—a level of authoritative respect. He felt Johnson was no longer in his corner and was not respecting the source of his paycheck. Jones got reports that Johnson was literally and figuratively rolling his eyes behind Jones's back, simple matters of boss/employee disrespect that become an issue when millions of dollars are involved and the entire sporting world is watching.

Besides, Jones has long believed there are no coaching geniuses in the sports world. Most teams that win in college and professional sports find the right person at the right time. A small number of coaches may make a noticeable difference in the years they win, but so much involves their ability to fit on-field talent within a given system. If the belief seems far-fetched, just consider the facts that say loudly and clearly that no one coach possesses magical winning powers to win every single season with any dealt hand. Winning, says Jones, requires several ingredients, including talent, management, coaching, and even a little luck.

The lesson is one he learned in Arkansas. Johnson, after all, left Dallas and eventually returned to coaching with the Miami Dolphins as a replacement for retiring legend Don Shula, who had won more than 65 percent of his games as head coach. In his first season, Johnson inherited a talented team led by quarterback Dan Marino that many people felt would challenge for the Super Bowl, but the team never came close to that goal. Johnson left after four seasons with just two playoff wins and a record barely above .500. Bill Parcells, who won two Super Bowls with the New York Giants, did not win a single playoff game as coach of the Cowboys despite having considerable talent. Bill Belichick had only one winning season as head coach in Cleveland, yet the man leads a modern-day juggernaut in New England, and former Dallas offensive coordinator Norv Turner never won as a head coach in Washington or Oakland but took San Diego to the AFC Championship Game in his first season with the Chargers in 2007.

"There are no gurus," Jones says. "No guru that can come in and say for sure, 'That's a great player.' It's so subjective. Most people look at talent due to comparisons of great players they've been with in the past."

Built around a parity system that distributes top draft choices to the worst teams and television money evenly to all the teams, including those in smaller markets, the NFL game is far bigger than the coaches and even the owners and general managers. Chemistry, then, is often the critical element when talent and solid coaching is in place, and Jones and Johnson were not working well together by the 1993 season. Jones was upset with Johnson's growing lack of patience with the owner, and privately, the owner was furious Johnson had insulted one of Jones's friends and team sponsors, an incident Jones still refuses to discuss publicly. The Dallas owner has long let those working for him know that if they want to really get him mad, try being rude to one of the Cowboys' key supporters.

The franchise was built in his era by stakeholders who helped balance a financial scale, and Jones had no intention of letting weight swing against his and the team's favor. He views his partners as necessary allies in the same way a college president views key contributing alumni. (Lesson, Arkansas.) So when Johnson insulted a Jones friend and a key Cowboys sponsor in 1993, Jones believed it was done on purpose to send him a message. He admits he did not do an effective job at managing Johnson as an employee, and the broken communication lines fostered an environment in which the coach had to send smoke signals by throwing a barb at a supporter he knew would report the slight back to Jones.

"Jimmy is smart," Jones said. "He knew what he was doing. He was right with you when you were losing, but winning changed everything. He was feeling pressure. I was feeling pressure. We all were."

The difference between the two, though, was that Jerry Jones owned the team and had a $40 million note at a bank in Texas while Johnson was drawing a guaranteed salary.

Says Jones, "Jimmy said to me, 'Do you have any idea the pressure I'm under?' I said, 'Well, you are trading my account.' Pressure is having a note due, knowing you don't have the money to pay it; knowing you have to go to the banker and ask for more money."

Johnson and Jones had become careless with their relationship amid the fast-paced, ego-boosting effects and distraction that came with winning and winning quickly. One was constantly trying to outdo the other, and therefore the question was constantly and distractingly asked by media and fans during the team's championship play: who deserves the credit?

Success had come so fast for the Cowboys that it resulted in natural relational problems common in celebrity and sport. The clinching blow for Jones and Johnson came at the NFL spring meetings in Orlando in March just two months after the second Super Bowl win, though the irreparable damage had probably already been done. Johnson was at a restaurant table, sitting with Bob Ackles, the former Dallas player personnel manager who by then worked for the Cardinals after previously being fired by Jones, and another former Cowboys employee, also previously terminated by Jones.

After a drink or two consumed during the cocktail hour, Jones walked up to the table, offering to toast all who had a role in helping Dallas win two Super Bowls, including Johnson and the former Cowboys employees. Response from the table was unenthusiastic at best and Jones was incensed, expecting that his current employee, at the very least, would kindly oblige with appropriate returning remarks. Dynamics of the relationship had changed from the days when Johnson was working hard to help Jones sell suites and Jones was eagerly taking his coach to NFL owners meetings.

Jones felt Johnson's snub at the table during the NFL meeting was insubordination and he struggled to control his anger. Johnson left the festivities while Jones went to the hotel bar and vented, letting his emotions fly. Several months of pent-up frustration in regard to Johnson came rolling off his tongue as the night wore on. The room was filled with journalists, NFL employees, and others enjoying the free-flowing conversation. Jones reportedly said that fateful night, "I should have fired him and brought in Barry Switzer. There are 500 coaches who could have won the Super Bowl with our team."

Responding publicly the next day, Johnson fired back, "I've heard from numerous reliable sources that he [Jones] was in the bar the early hours of the morning and threatening to fire me and said he was going to fire me at least eight or nine times."

Jones did not deny the dialogue, saying it was the "whiskey talking." He was upset at being quoted off the record but understands he bore responsibility for the transpiring events. Over the next several days, he and Johnson talked by telephone; Johnson made the initial call. Jones and Johnson discussed working together and how they might continue working together in the future, but ultimately Jones was not interested in Johnson being Dallas's coach through the remainder of his contract. The J and J relationship was causing too much stress to all parties involved. Jones believed the relationship had become strained to the point that he did not think Johnson could coach the team effectively with the obvious fragmentation. The magic was no longer there, taken away by the egos and miscommunication. So Jones structured a $2 million settlement for Johnson that effectively ended the remaining years of his original 10-year contract.

"I might have tolerated it [the changed dynamics] had we still been down on our knees," Jones says. "But I lost my tolerance. I sensed a lack of loyalty and I just did not see it [going forth]."

Days after the managerial epiphany, former University of Oklahoma coach and former University of Arkansas player and assistant coach Barry Switzer was announced as the new head coach of the Dallas Cowboys. Many team followers were surprised the relationship between Jones and Johnson had deteriorated so fast from the hungry days of 1989 to the finger-pointing days of 1993. Rich Dalrymple, the team's public relations director who worked with Johnson at Miami and was hired in Dallas in part so the coach would have a known and trusted entity to work, was angry at first when news of the breakup became apparent. Soon enough, however, he realized Johnson had never coached anywhere longer than five years besides Dallas, where he coached for five seasons. In his opinion, Johnson was getting restless. The Cowboys had a record run under the coach, and his tenure would have ended sooner rather than later anyway as he sought opportunity elsewhere. Johnson was burned out from the frantic pace executed from the moment he took the job, and going out a winner had its rewards.

In departure, Johnson might have been burned out, but he was hardly over the conflict with his old college roommate. The two had parted ways with a love-fest press conference that was filled with niceties, yet nobody really bought into it and in the days and months following Johnson's departure, he and Jones barely spoke. Johnson served two years as a Fox studio analyst before coaching the Dolphins for four years and then returning to Fox. It was not until the second year of his first stint as a television commentator that an overture toward patching the relationship was made. Two years after leaving Dallas, Johnson was back in town for a game. Before kickoff, Jones was on the sideline in front of the Cowboys bench. Johnson sought out his former boss and they exchanged a quick handshake and short pleasantries.

Closure, said Jones.

The right thing to do, said Johnson.

"It worked so great for us for five years, and we had things happen to us that were even better than we thought could happen to us," Jones said. "That is the way that I feel about it when I look back; we've known each other 30 years and those were the most intense times when we were working together for five years. It worked real well, and when you look at the little bumps along the way, they are so minimized by the great success that we've had."

Years would pass, however, before the relationship truly began to mend. In 2001, Johnson picked on Jones during halftime of a *Monday Night Football* broadcast, comparing his physical makeover to Michael Jackson. After his father died, Jones became more conscious about vulnerability and aging. He lost more than 50 pounds by implementing a rigorous daily exercise regimen and cutting back alcohol consumption. Jones dismissed Johnson's remark when asked about it, saying that was just "Jimmy being Jimmy." A turning point for the two came a couple of years later when Johnson was in Dallas handling the pregame broadcast of the annual Thanksgiving Day game for Fox. Johnson wanted a place to watch the evening game being broadcast on the NFL Network, so Dalrymple put him in a Texas Stadium suite near the Jones family suite.

After the game, Jones and his son, Stephen, walked next door to visit Johnson. They were all drinking beer, relaxing, laughing, and talking about good old days gone by. Johnson has since been back for championship team reunions, embracing his days as coach, and while he and Jones still debate when given opportunity what was and could have been, each recognizes the relationship was a marked and memorable time for both. For his part, Jones describes his time with Johnson as very rewarding. He wishes they had not been so careless with one another in the end, but says benefits from the time together are far too many to look back and see anything but positives.

Taking a Calculated Risk

Born in 1937 in Crossett, Arkansas, Barry Switzer gave new meaning to suggestions that Jerry Jones was raised on the wrong side the tracks. Switzer's father was a bootlegger and money lender who spent time in prison for his roughneck lifestyle. Switzer was a football star in high school, known for his ferocious, fearless play, which earned him a football scholarship to the University of Arkansas in Fayetteville. He graduated with a degree in business in 1960, returning one year later after a brief stint in the army to serve as an assistant coach for the Razorbacks under head coach Frank Broyles, his former mentor. Switzer's ability to get tough with young players earned him responsibility for Arkansas's freshman team. In those days, redshirting from varsity play was mandatory for first-year players, and head coaches wanted leaders to shape, mold, and keep their young talent out of trouble. Among the first players Switzer coached were Jones and Johnson.

Switzer remembered Jones as a "try-hard guy...exactly as you see him...a total extrovert, a promoter, a salesman who could look you in the eye and talk right through you." He never hesitated when the telephone call came from Jones to lead the Cowboys. Switzer had won and won big in college, leading the Oklahoma Sooners to three national championships (1974, 1975, and 1985). Switzer's forte as a college coach was recruiting talent in Texas and mastering the powerful wishbone offense. His hard-luck background gave Switzer a leg up on competitors in recruiting because he was not afraid to walk into any home in any neighborhood and promise a mother he would be a father figure for her child. But trouble followed Switzer at Oklahoma, and his reputation for running a renegade program finally cost him the job in 1989 when the program was placed on probation for recruiting violations. Switzer had been out of work for six years when his telephone rang with a call from Jerry Jones, seeking a replacement for Jimmy Johnson.

The hiring of Switzer was a move that, like several notable moves by Jones over his career, was scrutinized and debated endlessly. Those close to Jones, however, were not all that surprised. Jones has a history of loyalty, keeping close ties with former teammates and longtime friends. His public reputation may not always reflect that, since his notorious conflicts with Landry and Johnson made headlines, but people close to Jones know differently. He has low tolerance for insubordination but a high level of stickability with those who share respect.

Consider the story of Jones and Arkansas attorney Tom Mars. As an aggressive, 32-year-old lawyer, Mars led the $80 million class action lawsuit against Arkla Gas Co. that ultimately involved Jones and his former company, Arkoma. Like Jones, Mars is a University of Arkansas graduate known for his intelligence and business acumen. He graduated first in his law class and made the highest score on the Arkansas Bar Exam. In the lawsuit, Mars was a bitter enemy of Jones. After the battle was over and settlements were made, however, Mars was singing Jones's praises, talking about how the Cowboys owner never did anything illegal or inappropriate at Arkoma and that he really respected Jones. Mars and Jones found more common ground than not despite their onetime legal differences.

Jones, says one observer, has an ability to chip away at his objectors, usually finding a way to make amends before too many years pass. He can also quickly forget transgressions when believing they were made with the best intent. For example, when Brad Sham, host of Jones's weekly television show and the team's game announcer, said to a pregame listening audience in 1994 that Jones and head coach Barry Switzer sometimes lie when talking publicly about the Cowboys, Jones fired him as the show's host. The comment was a slip of the tongue by Sham, who meant Jones and Switzer may praise a player publicly while having different thoughts behind the scenes, but it did not come out that way. Still, Sham maintains his close relationship with Jones and the Cowboys today and continues as the radio voice of the team, a position he has held since 1984.

An old friend and trusted entity who had won big in college just like Johnson prior to his hiring, Switzer fit the mold of what Jones was looking for. Jones knew the former Oklahoma coach for more than three decades, knew Switzer could work well with players, and knew his old friend understood the basics of football, such as the length of a field and the requirements for getting one team into the end zone and keeping another out. Without a lifetime in the NFL and dozens of relationships to draw upon when he entered the league, Jones often turned to his old college contacts for coaches and football staff members simply because those were men he knew from firsthand experience. In addition to Johnson and Switzer, Jones hired longtime friend Larry Lacewell, a former college coach, as the team's scouting director.

When Switzer got the call, he was all but done in the business of coaching. He needed a break to get back into the game, so loyalty to Jones was never going to be a question. The Cowboys owner and general manager wanted a more amicable coach after the stressful Johnson experience, and the unemployed Switzer would have no reason to be divisive. Also, Jones says today that of all the coaches he has ever worked with, from Johnson to Bill Parcells, Switzer was among the best at analyzing talent, possessing an innate football sense that helped him identify players with that hunger coaches look for. Switzer might not have been the smartest coach to ever roam the sideline, and some qualities, such as a loose handling of the team from a disciplinary standpoint, made him a shaky fit in the NFL, but for Jones and

Selecting quarterback Troy Aikman with the first pick in the 1989 NFL Draft put Jerry Jones's Cowboys on the path to greatness.

Jones and head coach Jimmy Johnson won two Super Bowls before parting ways in 1994. (Photo courtesy of Getty Images)

The Cowboys were the first athletic team to visit newly elected president Bill Clinton at the White House following their victory in Super Bowl XXVII.

Jones announces the signing of All-Pro cornerback Deion Sanders on September 9, 1995. It marked the highest-profile signing of an NFL unrestricted free agent in league history.

Accepting the Lombardi Trophy with head coach Barry Switzer following the Cowboys' 27–17 win over Pittsburgh in Super Bowl XXX at Sun Devil Stadium in Tempe, Arizona, on January 28, 1996.

A visit to the Gene and Jerry Jones Family Center for Children in Irving, Texas. The center opened in 1998.

Nelson Mandela attends his first NFL game in the owners' box at Texas Stadium with Gene and Jerry Jones as Dallas faces Washington on October 24, 1999.

New Cowboys head coach Bill Parcells with Jerry and Stephen Jones on draft day in April of 2003.

Jones visits with Cowboys fans during a game against the 49ers in San Francisco.
(Photo courtesy of Getty Images)

Jones joins the "Triplets," Michael Irvin, Troy Aikman, and Emmitt Smith, after announcing that the famed trio would be inducted into the team's Ring of Honor in 2005.

Wade Phillips is given his first tour of the Cowboys' locker room after succeeding Bill Parcells as the team's seventh head coach on February 8, 2007.

Jerry Jones and his board of directors: sons Stephen and Jerry Jr., wife Gene, and daughter Charlotte Anderson.

Jones announces the signing of quarterback Tony Romo to a six-year, $67 million contract at the team's headquarters in Irving, Texas, on October 30, 2007.
(Photo courtesy of AP Images)

The Cowboys' new stadium in Arlington, Texas, will be the home to Super Bowl XLV on February 6, 2011.

the Cowboys, he was the right coach for the team at the right time. All they needed was someone to take the talent on hand and win another Super Bowl.

The challenge was becoming increasingly difficult, however, considering the Cowboys had 11 Pro Bowl players returning from 1993 and the franchise was beginning to have NFL salary cap issues due to excessive, bloated salaries for star veterans. Jones and Dallas had the league's highest-paid quarterback, the highest-paid fullback, the second-highest-paid running back, and another half a dozen stars near the top at their position in pay, so managing salaries and talent became more of an issue than ever before.

After Switzer's hiring, quarterback Troy Aikman praised the new coach, suggesting Switzer, whom he played under for one season at Oklahoma, was a winner. Outspoken receiver Michael Irvin was not so sure, though. He blasted Jones and Switzer not long after the hiring, saying he was angry at the "ego, personality, whatever the hell it was" that sent Jimmy Johnson running away from the Cowboys. Irvin also complained about his contract to members of the media, and Jones requested a meeting with his All-Pro receiver to try to get him in line with team objectives.

Controversy regarding Johnson's departure was nowhere near the level Jones and the Cowboys experienced over the Landry termination, but negativity was undoubtedly swirling. In the summer before training camp began, a magazine known for publishing highly critical articles ran a large feature story on Jones, showing the Dallas owner and general manager on the cover with devil's horns graphically attached to his head. One of the more notable assertions in the June 1994 issue of *Texas Monthly* was, "It's his [Jones's] team and he can do what he wants. And what Jerry Jones wants to do most is prove he can win without Jimmy Johnson."

The 1994 season was hardly the disaster many onlookers predicted would occur under Switzer's leadership. If anything, the Cowboys barely missed a beat from the previous year, rolling to a 12–4 regular-season record and clinching the NFC East title in early December with a 31–19 win on the road at Philadelphia. The Cowboys offense was as potent as ever, compiling more than 5,300 yards, and the team's defense was actually improved over the year before. Everything was running smoothly at Valley Ranch as controversy in the front office was almost nonexistent. Maybe the owner had a point. Maybe the Dallas Cowboys could win with Switzer, formerly an out-of-work college coach.

Switzer, for his part, was not going to get in the way of a good thing, in the beginning at least. Starting with training camp, Switzer yielded to Jones, understanding the role he was hired to fill: head coach. As the general manager and owner, Jones knew more about the personnel and the chemistry than he did, so Switzer was completely willing to coach and nothing more. No power struggles, just football.

With the team performing well, Jones was satisfied and quiet, relatively speaking. He was talking away from the field about expanding Texas Stadium, giving Irving a world-recognized showplace with 100,000 seats and interactive fan opportunities throughout. Life for the owner with two Super Bowl trophies already in hand was good. He and Gene moved out of their Dallas penthouse to a mansion built on five hidden acres in the prominent Turtle Creek neighborhood, and for the first time since buying the team Jones was catching his breath, spending more time on the bigger picture than minute relational details. He did not escape scrutiny, however.

Late in the season, Jones was taking heat from the league for delayed reporting of an injury to Aikman's thumb. League regulations say teams are obligated to report injuries and playing status early in the week before a game. Aikman had a bad thumb, but Jones did not submit an injury report because he said the quarterback was never in jeopardy of not playing and he did not want the team's next opponent, the 49ers, to know about the banged-up thumb. The NFL looked into the matter and fined Jones $10,000, but the Dallas owner and general manager was unfazed.

"The NFL looking into something has never influenced me," he said. "We'll do it again, no matter what the league says about it. And I'm very confident there is no issue as far as the NFL is concerned. He played."

The only major problem during Switzer's first season came when the Cowboys lost on the road to the 49ers in the NFC Championship

Game. Most NFL teams would be thrilled to win 12 regular-season games and lose a close contest in the conference championship, but a difficult precedent had been set the previous two years with back-to-back Super Bowl wins. Dallas had played superlatively, but with so much winning experience and talent on hand, close was not good enough. Jones knew he and the franchise had something to prove following the departure of Johnson. The Dallas owner was bound and determined to write a different ending to his ongoing gridiron saga the next season. The Cowboys absolutely had to win the Super Bowl in 1995. Anything short of the ultimate victory would not suffice.

Land the Brightest Star

Since San Francisco was one of the NFL's elite teams in the 1980s and because the 49ers repeatedly had the Cowboys' number on the field, some suggested Jones was obsessed with overcoming his NFC nemesis. Jones preferred to describe his interest in San Francisco as competitive attention. But not even Jones denies his attention paid to San Francisco contributed to his desire to be the best in the same way the NBA's Los Angeles Lakers felt about the Boston Celtics in the 1980s or the way golfer Phil Mickelson feels about Tiger Woods today. Jones's competitive nature—combined with the reality that Dallas had a flashy, ticket-selling offense but a not-so-star-studded defense—led him to woo 49ers free agent cornerback Deion Sanders before the 1995 season.

A flashy, jewelry-wearing defensive back from Florida State who played professional baseball as a second sport during the NFL's off-season, Sanders was not exactly in his prime in 1994, his only season in San Francisco. He was considered a malcontent, stirring up the clubhouse with words on a variety of controversial subjects, including the play of quarterback Steve Young. Nobody questioned Sanders's playing ability, but questions were plentiful about his coach-ability. Beyond that, as one of the highest-paid defensive backs in the NFL, he promised to seek even more money on the free market. Jones was intrigued from the start, undeterred by the cost of landing a star for his team's defense.

Jones's strategy to sign Sanders was no secret. San Francisco owner Eddie DeBartolo Jr. knew it; Stephen Jones knew it. And neither was in favor of the transaction. San Francisco had no interest in trying to pay the type of cash-on-the-spot signing bonus Sanders wanted (in excess of $10 million), and Jerry Jones's son had no interest in seeing the family business strained by what he termed a highly risky move. Financial fortunes had dramatically improved in Dallas following two Super Bowl wins, but with gross annual team revenues of less than $150 million in those days, writing such a large one-time check was not easy on the bank account. Furthermore, Sanders's high-dollar contract had the potential to handcuff the team in the future under the salary cap.

But Jerry Jones wanted to prove the Dallas Cowboys could and would win without Jimmy Johnson as head coach. Besides, he had already learned that showmanship in the NFL typically translated into financial, ticket-selling success, and Sanders trumped all other players in the game when it came to showmanship. So Jones talked multiple times with Sanders and Sanders's agent, selling the allure of playing for the Blue Star with the promise of a Super Bowl win in the package. Jones did not present the highest offer for the defensive back, but he had one of the best, guaranteeing a signing bonus of $13 million. Jones told his son Stephen what he had in mind for Sanders, and Stephen helped crunch the numbers to assess acquisition feasibility.

Signing Sanders to such a large contract was a terrible idea, Stephen told his father after looking at the numbers.

But I think he will make a difference, Jerry said in response.

We cannot afford him, Stephen said.

I can write that check, Jerry said.

But look what it will do to our salary cap, Stephen said.

I want to win now, Jerry said. I'm doing it.

The Dallas owner and general manager made plans to fly to Florida to meet with Sanders's agent and make the deal, rebuking the pleas of his son. Harsh words were exchanged between the father and son, the type of in-office battle that gets everyone's attention. Jerry admits he can bully his children in the workplace because he is their father and boss. He is completely cognizant of the fact and works on most days to give them due voice so decisions can be made together and wisely. The final call, however, falls under his charge, and in the case of Sanders, Jerry wanted the defensive back in a Cowboys uniform no matter what. He restructured the contracts of Aikman and Irvin to make room under the NFL's salary cap for Sanders and then flew to Florida to make the deal with Sanders's agent. Ultimately, Jones and the Cowboys agreed to a multiyear contract for more than $25 million, including a mammoth-sized $13 million signing bonus, the biggest for an unrestricted free agent in the history of the game at the time.

Specifically, the bonus was $12,999,999. The number 13 is Jones's lucky number, but Sanders had superstitions of his own and thus the deal was made for one dollar less. The small savings was not enough to ease the angst of Jones, who was thrilled with signing Sanders but realistic about the gaudiness of the numbers. When Jones, the man who helped work in his family's small-town Arkansas grocery store as a boy, committed to a $13 million signing bonus for a defensive back possessing a difficult-to-coach reputation, he did not do so without pause. On the flight back after sealing the deal, Jones told his pilot to make a stop in North Little Rock before heading back to Dallas. Jones was tired, having negotiated the contract in the dark of a September night from midnight until after 6:20 AM to get the deal done in time for the start of a new season. And he was emotional, in full awareness of the array of meanings and implications of his actions.

"The thought of writing that check [to Sanders] got my attention," says Jones. "I was flying home [after the meeting] and made a stop first in Arkansas. I went back to the house I grew up in and spent 30 minutes walking around the yard, looking around and reflecting, before flying back to Dallas. I wanted to make sure I had not lost it. I wanted to remember what that kind of money meant. Thirteen million dollars was a long way from where I came."

Challenge the Rule Book

"I did not buy the Dallas Cowboys because I wanted to make a dollar. I had dollars. I gave it up to buy the Cowboys. But once you get in you want to make it as viable and as good as you can."

—*Jerry Jones*

6

Challenge the Rule Book

Jerry Jones bought the Dallas Cowboys for a simple reason: he loves football and wanted to be an NFL owner more than any other professional aspiration. His primary objective from the beginning has been to win on the field. But once in possession of a valuable asset like America's Team, the businessman in Jones could not help but take over. Besides, the more money he is able to leverage from the Cowboys' brand of business, the more money he has to spend for the Cowboys' brand of football, including the enormous signing bonuses and the kind of flash and circumstance he believes elevates a relatively simple game into something much, much larger.

That is why after several years of franchise ownership, Jones went on a calculated mission to parlay the brand and business he owned into tangible opportunity. Jones became, according to *Fortune* magazine, "one of the most aggressive businessmen in the league," taking the view that sharing all revenue, as NFL owners had long done, was all well and good, but teams were leaving considerable revenue potential untapped, thereby confining the success of the NFL and its teams to a conservative, status quo mode of limited growth. Jones, in fact, saw unlimited potential and worked aggressively to fully tap into it even though the league's charter and many longtime league owners said it could not and should not be done.

Before Jones arrived in the NFL, owners saw the game as little more than a contest played on a field measuring 120 yards long and 53⅓ yards wide by 11 players on each opposing side. To make more money than league peers, one team had to best on-field competitors more times than the others, thereby selling more tickets to games and more beers, bags of popcorn, and souvenirs to attending fans. Otherwise, all teams, according to the NFL's long-standing revenue-sharing plan, generated exactly the same revenue. Dollars from television contracts are split equally among all teams, as are licensing fees for sponsorship rights. If Visa, for instance, is the official credit card of the NFL, then all league owners share equally in the endorsement.

Jones supported the concept, understanding balance resulting from sharing allowed small-market teams to compete with large-market teams, resulting in a parity-based league that thrives on its unique competitiveness. He possessed one major difference of opinion with the league and most of its owners, however. League licensing was one thing, but he owned the Dallas Cowboys, and, more importantly, he controlled Texas Stadium, which had nothing to do with the NFL outside of being a site where sanctioned games were played. Under his ownership and control, the Dallas Cowboys were one entity, Texas Stadium was another. Many owners did nothing more than rent their stadiums, but Jones had effective ownership control of the Cowboys' playing venue from day one, and he understood the asset was completely underutilized and wanted to do something about it.

To pay big signing bonuses like the historic one to Deion Sanders, he needed to find a way to generate more revenue. Jones was also paying long-term bonuses to his cast of stars including Irvin, Aikman, and Smith, the result of his working to keep the team together and under the league's salary cap in the 1990s. But he had to fork over more than $40 million in bonuses in 1995, and the only way to gather that type of cash was through creative sponsorship. In the early years, Jones picked the proverbial low-hanging fruit with the team, leasing more than 100 available Texas Stadium luxury suites in an astoundingly short time (considering just a few had been leased when he bought the team), but the Cowboys were now Super Bowl champions. Season tickets were sold out, luxury suites were sold out, and the league's television contract was set for several more years, capping potential revenue. Jones needed more money, simple as that, and he just happened to own an underutilized asset he could put to work in the endeavor.

Jones has long believed that opportunities often lie dormant in a businessman's hands, and the creative businessman need only look harder and closer to take advantage of them. He once went after holes considered dry in the oil and gas business and effectively struck gold. The Dallas Cowboys, with a globally recognized and beloved brand, were nothing close to a dry hole. But NFL Properties, which handled licensing deals for the league outside of television contracts, was paying just roughly $3 million a year per team in return for the total sum of its licensing deals in the mid-1990s. That amount would not land Deion Sanders or keep stars of his emerging Team of the Decade intact. "You have to be sound financially, whether it's a family or a business," says Jones. So he sought drastic change, effectively saying the aged NFL rules limiting opportunity be damned.

"I know that this son of a bitch," Jones told a journalist in 1995, "could be losing $25 million a year right now and I could be the laughingstock to the rest of the world. So you can't ever take from my mind what it was like for me when I danced with the devil to buy this ballclub. If the economy and the TV contract hadn't taken off and some of the other good things hadn't happened, there is no way the Cowboys would have come out of it."

Jones aggressively set about converting his brand into sponsorship dollars and wound up firing the financial shot heard around the NFL in 1995. Ultimately, he would rewrite the charter of the NFL, setting the league on a path of unprecedented strength and revenue. In the beginning, however, his big idea did not go over so smoothly.

"It's hard to apply this business to a balance sheet, but we work from emotion, tradition, and the competitive aspects that result in a unique brand," says Jones. "In the real world, it may not appear to be worth much, but I saw lots of intangibles and felt like we could do more with them to help the franchise."

The battle against NFL Properties began in August 1995, just before the start of a new season, when Jones conducted a press conference in Austin, Texas, during the Cowboys' training camp to announce with a touch of showmanship and flair that he was kicking Coca-Cola out from Texas Stadium, replacing the soft drink giant with Pepsi and

Dr Pepper products. Wearing a pair of white cowboy boots emblazoned on the side with a Pepsi insignia given to him by Pepsico, a standing Jones added theater to his announcement that Pepsi and Dr Pepper had signed a 10-year, $40 million contract with Texas Stadium to become the official drink of the Dallas Cowboys. Flinging his foot forward, Jones said he had kicked out Coke, the soft drink that held official sponsorship rights with the NFL. The photo of Jones kicking out Coke in his white Pepsi boots made newspapers around the country, spiking America's long-running cola war. The sponsor could not have been more pleased, getting immediate payoff valued far above the return of hanging sponsorship signs at Texas Stadium.

"It can't look scripted," says Jones, "and you can't legislate that in a contract. But I ask myself, *How would I like this asset used if I were them?* We are busting our butt to work [for the sponsors] and do more than they expect. Any coach I have understands; this is part of their deal, too. Fundamentally, it's about how you create the authenticity of being tied to the team."

When NFL commissioner Paul Tagliabue heard about the Cowboys' Pepsi contract, he said Jones was shortsighted and self-serving in his actions. Several weeks later Tagliabue was more visibly upset when appearing at an owners meeting after Jones had announced subsequent licensing deals that threatened the long-standing territory protected by NFL Properties. Jones had followed the Pepsi announcement with news of a $2.5 million-a-year deal with Nike, which did not have a contract with NFL Properties. In announcing the deal, Jones sent out a press release under the headline "Cowboys Owner Bucks N.F.L. Again" and "strode to his team's sideline with Phil Knight, the chairman of Nike, and Monica Seles, the tennis star and Nike endorser" before a nationally televised *Monday Night Football* game against the Giants in New York.

Weeks later, Jones announced a sponsorship deal with American Express—Visa, of course, was the league's official sponsor—and later signed up ACME as the official brick of the Cowboys. The NFL front office, including Tagliabue and NFL Properties president Sara Levinson, was irate and so were many team owners, particularly those who did not control their stadiums and therefore felt left out of a good thing. Pepsi, American Express, and Jones were amused—delighted even—but the league as a whole was not. Dallas was responsible for more than 20 percent of all NFL licensed merchandise sales. No other team was even close, including the popular 49ers, so the threat of Dallas pulling out of NFL Properties was daunting for the league.

San Francisco's Eddie DeBartolo Jr. heavily criticized Jones in response, publicly ripping his fellow owner. He suggested Jones's independent moves to make money for the Cowboys would eventually kill the league. "The league will die," he said. "Down the road, the league will die. We can't have people going out on their own and doing this. It's counterproductive. It's just not right."

The 49ers' president, Carmen Policy, concurred: "The man's gone too far."

Cleveland owner Art Modell was more direct, screaming into his car phone about Jones while talking to a writer with *Sports Illustrated*: "He's going to tear down this league, goddammit."

To stop the actions of its renegade owner, the NFL made an emphatic point by filing a $300 million lawsuit against Jones and the Cowboys in the U.S. District Court in New York. The league sought damages under the accusation that Jones had embarked on a "wrongful plan and scheme to destroy the structure and operations of NFL Properties in order to gain for the Cowboys more than an equal share of licensing revenue."

Publicly, Jones showed a stern face, but behind the scenes he was bothered by the conflict. He loves the NFL as much as any owner, if not more, so he did not enjoy the controversy. The league, he said, was bullying him. He, on the other hand, was just trying to boldly make a point because good business sense told him to. Legally, the NFL had no ground to stand on. Jones owned his stadium; the league did not. Therefore, he can license it to whatever company he wants. Also, he firmly believed that allowing teams to maximize their individual brand potential only benefited the league as a whole.

"The more you grow the pie," he said, "the more you grow the league. We would make the players and the teams more money if we were all responsible for our own marketing."

Among Jones's most vocal detractors was the late Giants owner Wellington Mara, who was instrumental years before in helping Pete Rozelle form NFL Properties. When Jones argued at an owners meeting that teams should control their own licensing, Mara reportedly said, "That's great, but if we do that, we should do everything like that. [Jets owner] Leon Hess and I will take back the New York market for television, and you can see what kind of TV contract you can get for the 16th-largest media market in the country." When Mara finished talking, many other owners applauded. But it was not that simple.

Television contracts belonged to the league. The Cowboys belonged to the league. But control of Texas Stadium belonged to Jerry Jones, just as control of Foxboro Stadium belonged to the Kraft family who owned the New England Patriots, and control of Joe Robbie Stadium belonged to Miami Dolphins owner Wayne Huizenga. The rest of the league's owners essentially rented stadiums for games. Thus, among the first breaks in the conflict for Jones came when the Kraft family followed his lead, announcing a five-year deal with Pepsi for their Foxboro Stadium. The sponsorship was critical in creating league support of Jones because, while he and Robert Kraft have been the fastest of friends throughout their time together as owners, Kraft was not viewed as an instigator the way Jones was.

To fight against the league and its $300 million lawsuit, Jones filed a $700 million lawsuit against NFL Properties, alleging its centralized role violated antitrust laws. By late November 1995, less than two months after the NFL filed its lawsuit, Tagliabue was backing off his harsh comments of Jones and his actions, talking about settling out of court. Jones, too, was relieved, ready to settle and move forward without conflict with his peers. For more than a year both sides negotiated settlement, but it was Jones who clearly won when the settlement was announced in late 1996, allowing him and other owners to independently handle team-specific licensing. "Score

Another Victory for Jerry Jones's Dallas Cowboys" proclaimed one newspaper headline.

"Money," said Stephen Jones, "is how a businessman measures success. In a way, accumulating money is keeping score. Jerry may not need more money, but if he doesn't make it, in his mind, he has failed. And to make it, he has to keep making his businesses better."

In the years following the settlement, most league owners have studied or duplicated at least some marketing aspects initiated by Jones, and most have implemented many. They watched and carefully took note of how the Cowboys owner parlayed his football team into multilateral brand strength and revenue. Never one to rest on its laurels, Dallas took its direct approach to licensing several steps further. The Cowboys, for instance, became the only team in the NFL to handle its own merchandise sales and licensing.

Unusual for professional sports teams, Jones and his Cowboys enterprise control all aspects of T-shirt and merchandise sales, providing millions in additional revenue considering Dallas is easily the league leader in merchandise sales. Control has its risks, of course. If they think the team is headed for a big year and order too much, they have to absorb the excess inventory. But the payoff can be high, particularly in winning seasons like 2007, and particularly when a star player like quarterback Tony Romo is excelling, considering the profit margin of owning the space versus earning a small licensing royalty is considerable.

To facilitate merchandise sales, members of the Jones family went to NASCAR events, inspecting the big souvenir trucks effectively used at the tracks. The Cowboys built several of their own at a cost of several hundred thousand dollars each. Fans attending training camp or home Cowboys games frequently line up at the enormous blue rigs full of authentic jerseys and T-shirts, making the investment look more like genius than risk.

"We go out and study," says Stephen Jones, the team's CEO. "We try to duplicate what works. The biggest problem [in handling all merchandising] is losing. But when you win, you cash in all bets. You've put the infrastructure in place to pay off and handle the up times."

Hands-On Leadership

Almost immediately Jerry Jones transformed from being a renegade owner to becoming a force to be reckoned with in the NFL. With expansion teams in Jacksonville and Carolina increasing the league's lineup to 30 franchises (Cleveland and Houston later raised that number to 32) and further diversifying the ownership base, Jones was earning the respect of many of his former objectors with undeniable results. So his strength among owners was increasing fast. Seeing, after all, is believing.

Jones developed camaraderie with many owners, often holding after-meeting gatherings in his hotel suite, where he and others discussed decisions and the future of the game over cocktails. And he earned a reputation for an array of distinguishing qualities, from giving the most profound speeches at meetings to being a man of his word. "When he comes and shakes your hand [on agreement], you never have to ask twice," says Bill Ford Jr., whose family owns the Detroit Lions.

Another Jones trademark, says Ford, are the passionate speeches and incessant lobbying among peers he conducts at meetings, doing so in a way that over the years warmed some of his original detractors from the league's old guard. Probably every owner has a Jerry Jones story after being on an opposing side in an issue, but none has denied he raises the league's energy level, pushing owners to seek new opportunities. John Mara, the Giants co-owner who took over leadership of the team following the death of his father in 2005, said Jones is both respected and admired by his peers—including the Mara family.

"Even my father at the end had come to enjoy him," said John Mara. "When Jerry got up to speak at a league meeting, my father would always perk up and give him a big greeting. He enjoyed Jerry. At the beginning, he didn't."

Many owners took to Jones from the very start of their relationship, such as Jerry Richardson, owner of the NFL's Carolina Panthers. Only the second former NFL player to own a team, Richardson made his money after a two-year playing career with the Baltimore Colts in the fast-food business as one of the largest and original owners of Hardee's. Like Jones, Richardson was a college football star, setting records as a receiver at South Carolina's Wofford College. And, like Jones, he is a self-made billionaire, known for his business acumen as well as personal warmth and sense of humor.

A football man and hands-on operational NFL boss himself since launching the expansion Panthers in 1993, Richardson joined Jones among the group of new-generation owners who quickly changed the face of the NFL landscape. With Jones's Cowboys winning Super Bowls and revolutionizing the franchise business model, his voice naturally became considerably stronger. Combined with other owners like Richardson and Detroit's Bill Ford Jr., the chairman of Ford Motor Company who began representing his family's ownership, league voting dynamics changed considerably. The new voices do not always agree, but the fresh blood brought open, engaging minds to the table and everything quickly changed from the earlier days when Jones was considered a renegade outsider.

Ford and Jones did agree on one issue during the first NFL meeting Ford attended in the early 1990s. The league was considering taking the tradition of Thanksgiving Day games away from Dallas and Detroit due to a movement put forth by Kansas City Chiefs owner Lamar Hunt. Ford barely knew Jones at the time but knew that Jones did not want to lose the game, which had been played in Dallas since 1966, excluding two seasons. Ford did not want to lose the game either, which had been played in Detroit since 1934, excluding three seasons during World War II.

"I'm walking into an ambush," recalls Ford, who was in his thirties at the time. "Here is Lamar, a legend and fixture. I went up to Jerry, not knowing him really. Jerry said, 'Let me take care of this.' He stood up and gave a speech. It was the first time I had heard him speak in a room like that. He could put to shame a Southern preacher. He's such a salesman. But there is always value [in what he says]."

Jones is well known among fellow NFL owners for passionate stances taken over the years on a variety of issues. During formal meetings and informal after-hours meetings when he and many peers gather to discuss in clubhouse style pertinent league issues of the day, Jones draws attention. Says Ford, "Every time Jerry gets up to speak, it is worth listening to. Jerry is a showman. He can spellbind the room."

Jones, however, does not always win the day. Some owners are jealous and others have not warmed up to his style. Usually, though, he makes valid points for the league even if other owners don't line-item agree, making Ford, Richardson, and others among his biggest fans because they see how he positively impacts the game.

"If we had 32 Jerrys in the NFL we would have anarchy," says Ford, laughing. "But he's absolutely fantastic. A lot of new owners coming into the league have tried to emulate Jerry. But you can emulate the obvious flamboyant parts without being able to emulate the substance underneath. There is only one Jerry."

Richardson, for one, clearly understands Jones has not made himself coach of the Cowboys, but he also knows Jones probably comes closer in contact than any NFL team owner to players and coaches and actual involvement in their daily and weekly routine. Thus, Richardson refers endearingly to Jones at NFL meetings as "Coach," as in, "Let's hear from you, Coach Jones."

Jones, who once accidentally referred to himself as "Coach" during an interview, is amused by the endearment but emphatic when pressed on the issue of whether or not he has ever called a play during a game as some have rumored and suggested.

"No!" says Jones, conclusively.

Take my word, he says.

"I have never called a play for the Dallas Cowboys."

Jones admits to mentioning a few play strategies to coaches during meetings away from the field, and he has even joked publicly over the years about play calling because he knows the sensitivity some people have over the issue. The Diet Pepsi Max television commercial that ran on TV networks nationwide in 2007 is perhaps the best example of Jones's humor about play-calling suggestions. In the 30-second spot, Dallas's offensive play-caller is fatigued, yawning as he sends in a play to Wade Phillips, standing on the sideline. Phillips in turn interprets the same yawn-called play to quarterback Tony Romo, who makes the same awkward play interpretation to offensive players, getting sacked in the team's confusion. In the commercial, Jones walks into the coaching booth after the disaster, disturbed by the Cowboys' sleepy offensive play-caller.

"Hey," Jones says in the commercial to the team's offensive coach, before taking the headset to take over play calling. "I'll take that. You take this," and he hands the offensive coach a Diet Pepsi Max, designed to wake him up with its peppy impact produced by ginseng and more caffeine.

The ruse is obviously a spin on Jones's pronounced, hands-on leadership style but not, he says, a reflection of reality. He knows football and loves football. But he understands the value of coaches and lets them do their job in terms of X's and O's. Personnel decisions are his ultimate responsibility, though coaches have considerable input. Play calling, however, clearly belongs to the coach, he says. If he does not think they can do the job, he'll make a change, but he's not about to do the job for them.

"There have been times people actually thought I called the plays," says Jones, surprised. "Have I? No."

Unlike most other NFL owners, however, Jones does sit in on team meetings during the week, goes into the locker room before and after games, regularly watches practices from the sideline, and sits in on offensive and defensive coaches meetings during the week. Most owners do not crave that level of involvement, yet Jones does admit to getting more intricately involved with a coach once.

Barry Switzer was in the midst of his second season, trying to help Jones prove that the team could win a Super Bowl without Jimmy Johnson; that there are no guru coaches with magical powers others do not possess. You have to be a good coach with a talented team and even then it takes some breaks along the way to win big. Consider Broyles from Jones's days at Arkansas. A legendary coach in the old Southwest Conference, Broyles looked like an underachiever when his talented team played .500 ball Jones's junior season, but he looked like a genius the next year when his talented team went undefeated, winning the Cotton Bowl and laying claim to a national championship. Switzer had won in college, and though he had been out of coaching for six seasons and had never coached in the pros, Jones figured he knew football, and the Cowboys were loaded with talent, so he could probably get the job done.

And he was right.

Switzer's first year was a success all the way down to the NFC Championship Game, which the Cowboys lost on the road at San Francisco 38–28. The team performed well under Switzer that season, sending 11 players to the Pro Bowl and notching 12 regular-season wins and a 35–9 thrashing of Green Bay in the divisional playoffs. The coach faced pressure in his second season, however, because he was under a close and watchful eye following Jimmy Johnson and his two Super Bowl wins. Only winning a Super Bowl himself would be enough, and in his first season the Cowboys came up short.

Switzer's reputation and demeanor with players was the exact opposite of Johnson's. Switzer was more relaxed with the team in terms of his intensity and rules. But he was not considered to have the same football acumen; he was more of a player's coach than an expert in strategy. So as pressure mounted on Dallas to return to the Super Bowl in late December 1995, pressure mounted on head coach Barry Switzer as well, and the strain showed.

The Cowboys were on the road at Philadelphia for a late-season division game, important in tying up home-field advantage for the upcoming playoffs. The week before, the team had lost a close game at Washington. Sports talk shows were lighting up the airwaves with voiced fear that Dallas would let its promising season slide away at the end without a coach like Johnson to guide the franchise down the homestretch. Philadelphia's Eagles featured a smash-mouth defense with heavy pressure on the ends, spelling trouble for the Cowboys' Troy Aikman. Jones was concerned about protection of his future Hall of Fame quarterback, who was beginning to show physical wear from several hard-fought years in the game. Jones met with Switzer and offensive coaches during the week of preparation and strongly suggested to Switzer that the Cowboys give up offensive production by leaving a running back in the backfield for extra pass blocking. With the playoffs looming and Dallas already assured a spot, protecting the quarterback was more important than points.

The game unfolded exactly the way Jones had envisioned, but Switzer and the Cowboys were using a different game plan than the one the owner had suggested. The Cowboys' running back was fleeing the pocket, seeking seams in the defense as a receiver. As a result, Aikman was getting clobbered without the extra blocker and Jones could not take watching the action. He left his seat in a suite and went down to the sideline, addressing Switzer on the field during the game.

"Did we not agree to leave a back in there?" said Jones, obviously incensed.

He ordered Switzer to change the strategy immediately, leaving a blocker in the backfield for quarterback protection.

"It [the move] minimized our offensive productivity and maybe it was out of bounds, but as the general manager, I did not want to lose my franchise quarterback before the playoffs and we were about to. I could not sit back and just watch it happen," explained Jones.

Intensity on the sideline and perhaps the pressure Switzer was feeling to win contributed to one of his most memorable blunders as coach. The game was close, a typical late-season NFC East slugfest. Late in the game, Dallas had a fourth-and-one from its own 29-yard line. Switzer kept the punter on the sideline, telling his offense to go for the first down. Such a move breaks almost every rule in the professional football coaching manual, which says to punt and get the ball back, but Switzer wanted to show aggression, that he wanted to win.

The play call was "load," a simple two-back set with a handoff to the second running back. The play did not work, but Dallas got a reprieve because officials had failed to stop it before the snap for the two-minute warning. Incredibly, the Cowboys ran the very same play again. Philadelphia made the stop, then kicked a short field goal moments later, winning the game 20–17. Switzer was called a bonehead in every corner of the football-watching world. Before the season, Jones had said anything less than winning a Super Bowl was unacceptable, and pressure on Switzer was piling high. But the former Oklahoma coach and his boss would get the last laugh of the season. Dallas went on a roll following the embarrassing Philadelphia loss, and receiver Michael Irvin actually labeled the fourth-and-one call as a positive turning point for the team.

Having his best season as a pro, Emmitt Smith rushed for an NFL-record 25 touchdowns and a team-record 1,773 yards for the season. Smith's play was critical for the Cowboys in the final stretch of the season, with two closing regular-season wins and two convincing play-off wins over Philadelphia (30–11 in the divisional round) and Green Bay (38–27 in the NFC Championship Game). The team reached the Super Bowl and beat Pittsburgh 27–17, becoming the first franchise in the history of the NFL to win three Super Bowls in four years. When Switzer was asked after the game about the win, he could utter little more than repetitive exclamation points.

"We did it!"

"We did it!"

"We did it!"

"I just want to say to Jerry Jones, 'Are you having a good time now, Jerry?' We did it," he said.

Jones was having a very good time, one of his professional best so far. The season had been long with the big victory seeming to take a lifetime to achieve after Dallas had come up short the year before. When you have won two Super Bowls in a row, 24 months is a long time to wait for another. And in Switzer's second season, turmoil was building internally among the coaches and players. Aikman did not agree with the coach's carefree disciplinary attitude, and he and Switzer were barely talking by the Super Bowl. As for Jones, after he had argued two years before that an out-of-work college coach could win a Super Bowl with his Cowboys, he felt immense pressure for the team to win. But Dallas did in fact get it done under Switzer, even if the coach could barely believe it himself.

"If anyone is willing to take a big risk, do his homework, and ask the right questions, you can be a success in anything you do," said Jones.

With the victory, Switzer became only the second coach in history to win both an NCAA championship and an NFL championship as a head man. The first person to do it, of course, was Jimmy Johnson.

Humility of the Game

"It's a very hard, unforgiving business. You've got to be on your toes, and you've got to be flexible, and all that does is give you a chance. Over time you get beaten up pretty bad."

—*Robert Kraft, owner of the New England Patriots*

7

Humility of the Game

Smiles do not last long in the National Football League. The hyper-competitive nature of the game, with team salary caps, structured draft choice distribution that rewards losing, and a plentiful share of the best talent and football tacticians in the world make winning big for several years in a row nearly impossible. That is why Dallas's three Super Bowl wins in four years was so important, earning the team the undisputed Team of the 1990s distinction. Some pundits went so far as to call it The Greatest Team Ever. But as with all dynasties, the Cowboys' pride certainly preceded the fall because, beginning in 1996, everything began to change and winning on the field became a considerably bigger challenge.

Immediately after winning Super Bowl XXX—in fact, shortly after walking off the turf of Sun Devil Stadium in Tempe, Arizona—Barry Switzer talked about the team's challenge in repeating as champions. The Cowboys faced significant roster changes due to free agency, and its collection of returning stars was aging.

"We won't be as good next year as we are this year," said Switzer.

Among the more surprising revelations in the moments after the Super Bowl win was that Jones, always the optimist, agreed with Switzer, saying, "We'd like to think we have positioned ourselves to continue to challenge for the Super Bowl. But we know we will have to suffer some hits."

Jones knew better than anybody else, of course, that the historic run had come because he had faced and made a critical choice in the years before. Win big while you can and pay the price later, or prepare for the future and risk never winning big at all. Anybody who knows anything at all about Jones understands the options were never debated whatsoever. When victory is at hand, grab it. And so he did. But the Lombardi Trophy that comes with winning the NFL's most coveted prize was barely out of his hands for the third time before he was facing that inevitable, dreaded future.

Problems were many as the team began its eighth season in the Jones era. Most notably, the top 15 Cowboys stars were scheduled to earn more than $30 million when the league's total salary cap for the year was roughly $40 million. To fill out a 53-man roster, somebody had to go or else minimum-wage rookies would have to take the rest of the team's spots. Nor did it help that Jones and company learned some of their most valuable lessons during the previous year's draft. Back in the spring of 1995, hoping to help the team continue on the strength of its stars, Jones and team scouting director Larry Lacewell, his old college teammate from Arkansas, decided on a unique strategy of drafting backup and special-teams players. They were not seeking starters, since Dallas already had an expensive team of stars in place.

The Cowboys selected guard Shane Hannah from Michigan State in the second round of the 1995 NFL Draft, a move that shocked even the player himself, who told reporters he never expected to go before the fifth round, if then. Hannah was on the roster for two seasons and never reached the playing field before being released. And Dallas selected safety Charlie Williams of Bowling Green in the third round that year while most teams considered him undrafted free-agent material. Williams remained on the Cowboys roster for several years but was never a starter. Nor was first-round pick Sherman Williams, a fumble-prone running back from Alabama released after five seasons.

"To get better at something, you have to look at your mistakes," said Lacewell, two years after results from the failed experiment became obvious. "Well, we certainly made some mistakes in that draft. It's there. You can't run from it."

The problem with so many Cowboys stars becoming free agents, including offensive tackle Erik Williams and defensive players Ken Norton, Tony Casillas, and James Washington, was that in restructuring the contracts of eight players the year before to sign Deion Sanders, Jones could not renegotiate those for another year according to league rules. He had no choice but to let pieces of his championship team go—the price of winning a third Super Bowl. Jones was able to keep most of his aging offensive stars together, but the defense lost a handful of talented, unrestricted free agents including tackle Russell Maryland, outside linebacker Dixon Edwards, and cornerback Larry Brown.

"But he [Jones] did the right thing," said Charley Casserly, the former general manager of the Washington Redskins. "You have to win it while you can, when you have a shot. These chances don't come around very often and you can't blow them."

Trouble of a different kind began soon after the Super Bowl when Irvin, the team's star receiver, was arrested in the spring on charges of drug possession at a hotel party where he was celebrating his 30th birthday. Rumors had swirled for some time that a few Cowboys, including Irvin, were living raucous lives, frequenting strip clubs and hanging around suspicious characters. Still, the arrest was a significant blow to the team because after multiple court appearances and dozens of newspaper and television headlines, Irvin pleaded no contest to the charges of marijuana and cocaine possession and was suspended by the NFL for the first five games of the 1996 season.

In Irvin's absence, the team struggled, losing three of its first four games. The Cowboys moved defensive back Sanders to wide receiver to try to make up for the loss of Irvin, but Sanders struggled and was no more than a token threat. Turmoil inside the team was growing as the bad-boy reputations of some players were blamed on the no-discipline style of Switzer and in contrast with the less-extravagant style of quarterback Troy Aikman. Jones was continually asked by the media about Switzer's job security even though he was less than a year removed from winning the Super Bowl. To try to calm the media storm that was only fueling controversy, Jones took a lawman's approach to reality and rumors, hiring off-duty police as security to patrol team facilities and make sure his players were not spending time off the field in the wrong places.

When Irvin finally returned, the team performed better, but he was hardly his old All-Pro self, garnering 962 yards receiving in 11 games. The Cowboys were further hurt by a bone spur slowing down Emmitt Smith. With diminished threats, Aikman threw only 12 touchdowns. Still, the team won 10 regular-season games and made the playoffs, beating Minnesota 40–15 in a Wild Card game before bowing out to the Carolina Panthers the following weekend. The Cowboys had more players selected to the NFC Pro Bowl (nine) than any other team and showed signs that all was not lost in Dallas. That quickly changed at the beginning of the next season, however.

Jones brought Switzer back as coach in 1997, but it was without a customary contract extension. The owner and general manager had more than a little concern over increasing signs that Switzer's anything-goes coaching style was allowing some of the team's players to run wild, losing focus on their professional obligation. The team was suffering a public-relations nightmare, earning a reputation as the NFL's bad boys. Some pundits and fans went so far as to blame Jones, suggesting that he did not follow the rules of the NFL so his players could not be expected to follow the rules of the team. In response, Jones hired former Dallas player Calvin Hill and his wife to monitor the behavior of the team. Jones also installed surveillance cameras in the training-camp dormitory and had plainclothes officers follow players walking through the Austin, Texas, bar district at night, making sure of their whereabouts and actions.

Dallas's reform effort received a setback before the season when Switzer was arrested for carrying a loaded handgun at Dallas–Fort Worth International Airport. He said it was a mistake, but Jones fined the coach $75,000 for a lapse in judgment. With Switzer being known as a whiskey drinker who loved a late-night party himself, his arrest only contributed to concern that he was running a team that knew no boundaries. Star offensive guard Nate Newton was facing sexual assault charges, and at the end of training camp, several unnamed players ripped down a security camera and caused damage to the dorm, urinating in a hall and damaging carpet and ceiling tiles. The team's stars were aging, its coach was under fire, and players were acting anything but professional. For the first time, Jones began to wonder out loud, albeit not completely seriously, if he should just take total control, serving as owner, general manager, and coach. As it became obvious Switzer could no longer get the team to respond, Jones stepped up his presence, putting the Cowboys through two-a-day practices, unheard of in the regular season in the NFL, and addressing the team about weaknesses.

"There are just too many coaches who have the experience to get it done better than I could," Jones said. "But there is something in me that would like to coach. I don't back away from that at all. I don't shy away from that. I consider it sometimes, yes. But first and foremost I want to be successful and not selfish, and the best chance for this organization to win is by having a full-time head coach who is qualified, so that's why I probably won't do it."

One thing quite clear was the fact that Switzer would not be coaching the Cowboys much longer. The coach had lost control of the team, which was struggling amid drastic personnel changes and a general lack of self-control. For a couple of seasons, he had been the right coach at the right time, an easy answer to a tumultuous period. His charge had been to win another Super Bowl and in 1995 he had delivered. But by late in the 1997 season, all signs made it clear that Switzer, 60 years of age, was about to be an unemployed coach once again. The Cowboys ended the year with five straight losses, missing the playoffs for the first time since 1990.

Almost immediately after the season, Switzer resigned. As a coach, he had compiled a .625 winning percentage, leading Dallas to that one all-important Super Bowl win. Unlike the Jimmy Johnson era, this coaching relationship ended amicably, despite the move coming at the insistence of the owner. Both Switzer and Jones knew the time was right, so the franchise moved unceremoniously on, the only question being who the next Cowboys coach would be.

Looking for Answers

Head coaches had been a source of frustration for Jones from the very moment he made a deal to buy the Dallas Cowboys. First, Tom Landry was a problem because his unceremonious firing created such a storm of controversy. Then, winning big created a poisonous atmosphere between Jones and Jimmy Johnson. After that, the inability to manage with a firm hand made Switzer's job more difficult than it should have been in Dallas. One can understand why, then, Jones lost some balance in regard to the owner/coach relationship for a few years afterward. He did not believe being the head coach should be so difficult, but because Jones had won more quickly and more often than anyone could have imagined, a high bar was set in terms of success by which to judge all others.

Of all the names bandied about in the media following Switzer's departure as to who might be the next Dallas coach—a list that included Washington Redskins head coach and former Cowboys offensive coordinator Norv Turner and San Francisco 49ers coach George Seifert—Chan Gailey was not one of them. The former Florida quarterback and college head coach who had served as offensive coordinator of the Pittsburgh Steelers was a dark horse if there ever was one. But Gailey had coached for four years (1979–1982) in the collegiate ranks with Ken Hatfield at Air Force. Hatfield coached Stephen Jones when he played at Arkansas and gave Gailey high marks. Also, Gailey was offensive coordinator of the 1997 Pittsburgh Steelers team that won 11 regular-season games and lost in the conference championship game to the Denver Broncos 24–21. His reputation was not for dynamism but for consistency and the technical aspects of the game. Not overly lax, not overly strict, Gailey was right down the middle. The problem was, following the headline-a-minute eras of Johnson and Switzer, Gailey was almost too nondescript for the bigger-than-life Blue Star.

For two years, the Dallas Cowboys played relatively well under Gailey, though. His first season, 1998, looked promising throughout the regular season. The team's offense, behind the improved running of a healthier Smith, rolled up more than 5,400 yards. Aikman made peace with troubled wide receiver Irvin and football's famed triplets were ever so briefly in business again. The only problem was that due to the free agency departures, Dallas's defense was porous, giving up almost as many yards as the offense generated. The team did win 10 games, sweeping all eight division games and reaching an NFC Wild Card game, but home-field advantage was not enough as the Cowboys lost their most surprising game in more than a decade, dropping a 20-7 heartbreaker to the usually inept Arizona Cardinals. The loss stung the once-proud franchise, sending a strong message that the dominating days of the 1990s were nearing an end.

Dating back to the franchise's years in Chicago and St. Louis, Arizona had not won a playoff game in 51 years. The team earning its first playoff win in half a century at Texas Stadium, against America's Team, got the attention of everyone in attendance, especially Jerry Jones. He remembers entering his owner's suite as the final seconds ticked off the clock in the loss to the Cardinals and seeing the faces of concerned family members including his wife, Gene, and daughter, Charlotte. At the time, Dallas had been in more playoff games than any other team in the NFL, and this might have been the worst—no, it was the worst—of the previous 51 appearances.

Dallas had beaten the Cardinals twice in the regular season and both times rather easily. But in the playoff game, the rhythm was off; the magic was not there. Aikman threw three interceptions. Smith carried just three times in the second half, nursing an injury. Led by quarterback Jake Plummer, Arizona was poised while Dallas was rattled. Fans uncharacteristically booed their beloved Cowboys. In his owner's suite, Jones turned to his wife and daughter, teeth tightly clenched as the clock expired, giving them a warning.

"Get ready," he said. "Get ready. We are really going to get it now."

Because Jones is highly visible in his role as owner and general manager of the Dallas Cowboys, he is the biggest and easiest target for criticism. He understands this, of course, and is willing to take the lumps that come with visibility, but that does not mean he likes it. The Jones family has endured over the years everything from rude heckling in restaurants to outright physical threats, but the period following the loss to Arizona was undoubtedly one of the worst. He was accused of dismantling the great team he had assembled, and few were interested in real stories of NFL salary caps and draft choice distribution that forced most of the change.

For Jones, the timing was particularly bad because he was emotionally distraught over the death of his father. Three years before, his father had fallen gravely ill while duck hunting with his son in Arkansas. Due to a congestive heart condition, which he had suffered from for years, Pat Jones's body was shutting down. Doctors said he would not live, but Jerry would not accept the prognosis. He took his father to other doctors, seeking the best care possible. When one suggested a risky operation, Pat agreed, having it in 1995. The surgery worked, giving Pat a couple more years of life. By the end—he died in late November 1997—Pat was weak and struggling to stay alive. Jerry had already resolved his father's business affairs, selling off his Exotic Animal Paradise business, located outside of Springfield, Missouri, but he was not ready for his departure. When Pat died at the age of 76, son Jerry was ill-prepared. Amid the turmoil and stress, he made a lifestyle change. Jones began working out rigorously, a routine that has not stopped. He gave up "cheeseburgers and beer," devoting an hour or more a day to exercise. He lost in excess of 50 pounds, weight he has not regained years later.

Getting in shape in his fifties amid the sobering death of his father was one thing. What so many people did not understand was his willingness to remain at the forefront during his team's struggles. Many owners get a photo taken when their team wins the Super Bowl, but how many go on talk radio shows and continually meet with the media and make multiple personal appearances when the franchise is losing? Among the first to suggest to Jones he take a quiet backseat was the wife of Clint Murchison, the previous longtime Cowboys owner. She once told Jones life would be a lot easier if he remained in the background as her husband had. But Jones does not believe a business owner should be absent. Also, he believes fans get far more in entertainment value when management has a face, a page he took from the book of Tex Schramm.

"I can't [step back], though maybe I should since in sports you can't win all the time, particularly with the [salary] structure of this league," he says. "Because when you step back and create barriers from the responsibility, you cut the fans out in many ways. Part of my role is niche management and part is niche ownership, and I like to let the fans be a part of it all through me."

Coaches have to be guarded in what they say. So do players, usually. As the owner and general manager, Jones can, and does, say whatever he feels. While players and coaches change over the years, in the two decades he has owned the Dallas Cowboys his image has been a constant. Jones understands that comes at a price. Some won't like it, of course, and he will be an easy target for harsh criticism, but Jones believes the value added outweighs the risk. He does not enjoy attack, especially when out of order in a public place or unfair, like the "complete undermining of credibility" he got upon buying the team. He does, however, understand it comes with the territory and does not want to change his style, believing it is best for the team and the game. Family members in turn accept some degree of criticism, recognizing the price has to be paid. Each just tries to disconnect it from their personal life, leaving criticism at the office.

"I can turn it on and off," says Stephen. "When I go coach my son's football game, for me, it's turned off. What someone says in the paper each day is not going to stop me. If they say Jerry is an idiot on a talk show one day, I'm not going to stay home and skip my next [scheduled] event. You just have to be even keel.

"Jerry has always set an example. A lot of it is trial and error. In the early years, he thrust himself into that [public] role and learned along the way. His big deal is not to hold a grudge against some writer or some fan for saying negative things. He does not blackball people. With us, he might throw a chair complaining about how he was treated, but with [the critics] he will take the high road. Ultimately, most come around and show more respect in the end."

The secret for Jones is getting face time with critics. On camera and in print, perhaps, ego may come across as a defining characteristic because he holds nothing back in opinion and does enjoy ongoing, sometimes long-running banter. He understands that he often talks too much and works in the proper setting to hold onto words, letting others speak. But given a microphone and a room full of questioners, he can talk and then some. What surprises most who get close to Jones, though, is that like most public personas, reality and appearance are often not in sync.

In the early days, certainly, several members of the Dallas media had endless fun at the owner's expense, poking at everything from his dialect to his run-on sentences to his excitability. But after he won them over, they and the rest of the throng came to have an unusual admiration for their most colorful subject. Ask journalists off the record whether they like Jerry Jones and one and all do very much. Just as Wellington Mara came around, so too do journalists and other detractors once they really get to know Jones. He is a family man who loves a good story and enjoys making interpersonal connections. Face-to-face he breaks down many misconceptions.

Jones is not about to deny that ego is a part of his persona. But most corporate leaders and members of the *Forbes* 400 list of the richest Americans have some degree of ego; his just happens to be a bit on the high side because he is always talking about what he and the team can and will do, and he is constantly on television or on the radio or in the newspaper where his confident personality is on display. Much of it comes from effort, though, because Jones believes the public does not want to hear him whine. Therefore, he takes a strong, proactive approach whenever he is in the public eye.

"You are what you are and I couldn't do it without being an optimist," says Jones. "I think because you're what you are, that an optimistic attitude literally, tangibly makes things happen. I think a negative attitude can tangibly make some things happen.... So by nature I come out of the shower optimistic. I go in that shower sometimes so low, lower than a crippled cricket's butt. Now all I'm trying to say...is that it is not natural to be optimistic all the time. I work on that. I really work on that real hard. So I do it to help maybe things move along."

Before Chan Gailey's second season as Dallas's coach, Jones suggested, as he does before every season, that the Cowboys had a chance to advance deep into the postseason. The ball did not bounce that way, though, as an 8–8 season in 1999 barely got the team into the playoffs, and then Dallas promptly lost in an NFC Wild Card game at Minnesota 27–10. The year was marked by Michael Irvin's career-ending neck and back injury that occurred in the fourth game of the season, a 13–10 loss at Philadelphia. After the playoff loss, Jones ended Gailey's tenure as coach after just two seasons. Gailey had an 18–14 regular-season record, but two consecutive playoff losses did not look like much for a team used to winning Super Bowls.

"I understand it's my responsibility," Gailey said. "It just didn't work out."

Jerry Jones liked Dave Campo, the coach who served on Switzer's staff during the Super Bowl season and as defensive coordinator under Gailey, because he was a quintessential football man, a generally unflappable technician of the game able to clearly illustrate game plans and focus on the X's and O's. The question was whether Campo was head-coaching material. One school of thought suggested he was better wired as a top-notch assistant coach, the kind who excels on the practice field more than in the media room or delivering the pregame speech. But Dallas has a unique way of giving its coaches a mystique, and Jones was still in a bit of an experimental mode, seeking the right mix to get the Cowboys back to the Super Bowl, so he took a chance on Campo, elevating the assistant to head coach.

"Jerry has the sense to step up when he feels he has to," said long-time friend and former Cowboys director of college and pro scouting Larry Lacewell. "Maybe he's not always right, but he always steps up, always pulls the trigger. He has taken more gambles than anyone I know. His whole life is a gamble, one big risk after another. But it's not done without research, without asking or listening to every single person he could possibly listen to."

The team had an insurmountable problem, however, with a low overall talent level as free agency and the decline and aging of its former stars kicked in completely. Aikman, the future Hall of Fame quarterback, suffered two concussions during the 2000 season. His absent and diminished play combined with a lack of depth provided a weak framework that no coaching change and no amount of optimism could overcome. Dallas finished the season with a 5–11 record, releasing Aikman due to salary cap concerns. When no other team picked up the quarterback, he retired, entering the broadcast booth as a color analyst.

With Aikman's sudden departure, Dallas had no quarterback replacement. No Danny White–style backup was waiting in the wings like the Cowboys had when their first great quarterback, Roger Staubach, retired. Including the preseason, Dallas had not one, not two, but *five* quarterbacks try their hand behind center during the 2001 season, including rookie Quincy Carter, Anthony Wright, Ryan Leaf, and Clint Stoerner. Running back Emmitt Smith was still able to move the ball, rushing for more than 1,000 yards for the 11th consecutive season despite weary legs. Jones was hopeful, suggesting the team could win 10 games, but Dallas finished 5–11 for the second consecutive season and in the NFC East cellar.

An air of optimism hovered around the team once again in 2002 as Jones spent millions in the off-season to upgrade the team's roster, providing more starters and more backups on both sides of the ball. Tired of losing, Jones wanted to do something about it, immediately, acquiring linebacker Kevin Hardy, defensive tackle La'Roi Glover, cornerback Bryant Westbrook, and tight end Tony McGee among others to fill big lineup holes. In the draft, Jones and the Cowboys selected defensive back Roy Williams, who some experts compared to former NFL great Ronnie Lott.

"It's understandable to have some down times, but it's inexcusable to let them continue for any length," said Jones.

The team conducted training camp at the Alamodome in San Antonio before the inquiring lenses of HBO, which recorded a documentary on the event. Running back Emmitt Smith entered the season needing only 539 yards to break Walter Payton's all-time career rushing yards mark of 16,726, and midway through the season cameras flashed in Texas Stadium as Smith broke free for an 11-yard run early in the fourth quarter against Seattle to get the record. The milestone would be the sole highlight during another disappointing season, however. Late in the year, with playoff hopes still barely alive, Dallas hosted San Francisco in a home game. The contest was one the Cowboys expected to win, turning the corner for a strong finish. The previous two weeks, the team had shown a spark, beating Jacksonville (21–19) and Washington (27–20) at home. A run to the playoffs seemed possible. Late in the fourth quarter against the 49ers, Dallas held a 10-point lead and appeared on its way to winning three straight games for the first time since 1999 as the Texas Stadium crowd of 64,000 roared in approval.

But the end of the game was a disaster, with questionable coaching decisions and tentative play plaguing the Cowboys' finish. Moments after Dallas took its 10-point lead, the Cowboys had a special teams breakdown, giving San Francisco a 42-yard kickoff return that set up a quick score. With little more than two minutes remaining, Campo decided to let his weakest field-goal kicker beyond 40 yards try a 47-yard attempt that would have given Dallas a 30–24 lead. He missed. And with 15 seconds remaining and the 49ers needing a score, the Cowboys ran a defensive scheme that forced seldom-used cornerback Dwayne Goodrich into man-to-man coverage with receiver Terrell Owens, one of the NFL's best. Owens caught an eight-yard touchdown pass and Dallas lost a heartbreaker as San Francisco clinched the NFC West title.

Outside of the Dallas locker room after the game, a visibly upset Jones had very few words to say to inquiring reporters. He briefly ranted before turning and walking off. "That was a stupid [expletive] ballgame," Jones said from a stairwell in the stadium's bowels. "The players played well enough to win. We [expletive] it up."

Losing, Jones says, is more difficult than he ever imagined. One loss does not prepare you for the next. If anything, he says, each one makes the next one more difficult. You never want to get comfortable coming up short. The more it hurts, the more you want to avoid it the next time. So the Cowboys owner and general manager has never made any apologies about having difficulty in handling defeat. He is playing the game to win and anything less is a disappointment. Thus, he cringes with every unnecessary penalty, every unforced fumble, every coaching blunder, and every obvious personnel deficiency.

Jones is quick to take the blame as well, saying he has "a legal pad full of mistakes" he's noted through the years. Many of them occurred during the driest seasons, the years bookended by Gailey and Campo, when the roster-depleted Cowboys had hit rock bottom and had trouble getting back up. He could have drafted better. He could have managed the coaching situation better. Jones thought Dallas had plugged its leaking holes, but he found there were far more than he had suspected. Frustration set in deeply. Tickets were still selling, but the franchise was having to work much harder to keep fan interest, spending more on marketing and ratcheting up the public relations machine to generate stories in an era when no headlines compared with those the team had generated years before. Merchandise sales, accounting for more than $50 million in annual revenues at the time, were slipping as well.

"I thought it [ownership] would be somewhere between playing at a high level and the excitement of attending games as a fan," says Jones, reflecting on the pressures of the NFL. "But it's much different. You feel every miscue. You see ghosts of the franchise going down on every bad play. Or you are wondering, *What is going to be written about us now?* when you lose?"

At the end of the 2002 season, after Dallas lost its final four games, finding its way to the bottom of the NFC East once again with a third consecutive 5–11 record, Jones decided enough was enough. A drastic new direction was in store for the Cowboys.

Change the Culture

"Is he [Jerry Jones] striving to build a statue of himself? No. He is driving for success. And someone else can build the statue."

—Mike McCoy, *former business partner of Jerry Jones*

8

Change the Culture

In football, as in life, one can never say never with any assuredness. What seems impossible sometimes happens. Just ask the 18-0 New England Patriots, who lost Super Bowl XLII to the underdog New York Giants. Yet even the most seasoned, open-minded veterans of the game trained to expect the unexpected could not have foreseen events that transpired in Dallas as Dave Campo's tenure as head coach came to an end.

With three weeks remaining in another dismal season, the Cowboys were getting dismantled on the road by the New York Giants, losing 37-7. The lethargic defeat in 2002 was perhaps the smoke everyone was looking for to signal that Campo would be relieved of his duties at the end of the year. Jones had planned to wait until the end of the regular season to analyze the situation, but right after the Giants game he got an unexpected phone call that quickly charted an entirely different path. ESPN reporter Chris Mortensen told Jones that colleague Bill Parcells was interested in coaching the Dallas Cowboys. (Interestingly, Campo returned as a Cowboys assistant coach in 2008.)

Working as a studio analyst for ESPN after retiring from coaching in 1999 following a particularly frustrating 8-8 season with the New York Jets, Parcells, nicknamed the Big Tuna, had watched Jones on the TV screen following the team's crushing loss to the Giants. At another time, Parcells had coached the Giants, earning a reputation after leading the team to two Super Bowl wins as one of professional football's all-time greatest coaches. Yet the coach had also earned a reputation as one of professional football's most domineering figures, possessing a controlling, dictatorial style, which made his interest in

Dallas surprising because of Jerry Jones's close involvement and strong personality. That is why Mortensen could hardly believe his ears in the studio when Parcells, after watching Jones on TV, uttered the words, "I could work for a guy like that." Parcells became a coaching legend after he took charge of the 1983 Giants, a team that had only one winning season in the previous decade, and led the team to Super Bowl wins in 1986 and 1990, retiring after the second title due to health concerns. He made a coaching comeback two years later with the New England Patriots but found frustration because he wanted more input into player personnel decisions. After four seasons and one Super Bowl loss, he left due to disagreements with owner Bob Kraft. His term as head coach of the New York Jets for three seasons was equally frustrating, and after never leading the team to the Super Bowl, Parcells quit, vowing to never coach again. But on that day he watched Jerry Jones on television following the Cowboys' dismal loss to the Giants, something moved his dormant coaching instinct, telling him, of all things, to get back on the field and lead a resurgence of the Cowboys.

Jones was surprised, naturally, when he received the call from Mortensen relaying Parcells's interest. Jones was known as a controlling owner and Parcells was known as a coach who craved control. On the surface, the relationship did not seem like a fit; on the other hand, Parcells was a seasoned football coach who had won at the highest level and was respected at almost every level. If he wanted to coach the Dallas Cowboys, Jones figured he better check it out. Several weeks remained in the season, but by then it was apparent to Jones that Campo was out. Jones picked up the phone and called Parcells to discuss the job, but not before he rationalized every conceivable side of the situation. He recalled thinking the relationship could be incredibly rewarding for the franchise yet also incredibly challenging.

"It would be recognition on my part that I needed to embrace a very strong opinion and a very strong individual," says Jones. "I went through the process of saying to myself, *Can I embrace that? Can I work in that climate?*"

Jones consulted his family, as is typical when such major decisions are at hand. He is not the only one who has to work with the team's head coach, of course, and the others have endured the ups and downs of Jerry's relationship with the coaches. Jones's wife, Gene, wanted Parcells; Jerry Jr. wanted Parcells; and Charlotte wanted Parcells. As the team's CEO, it was Stephen Jones who had the most to say about Parcells, telling his father the move was one he should make.

Definitely!

"You hit some home runs in business when you take risk," Stephen told his father. "But when you've taken a risk three times [on coaches] and you've had three losing seasons in a row, you don't need to take any chances. It was time to take the sure shot."

Jerry listened closely. The scale was tilting in Parcells's favor. The Cowboys owner and general manager boarded his jet, flying to meet the job-hunting coach in New Jersey. To avoid being seen, since Campo was still the coach under contract, they met on Jones's plane for lunch. The meeting was scheduled for an hour or so, but it took most of the day as both Parcells and Jones were captivated by the opportunity. Each liked the other more than they thought they would. The strangest union of all suddenly felt completely comfortable. The Cowboys went from having one of the lowest-paid head coaches in the league in Campo, who earned $500,000 per year, to one of the highest when Parcells signed a four-year, $17 million contract.

"Bill solicited the job," Jones says, "but I did not hesitate because I needed to demonstrate that I could work with a coach like him. I felt like the fans needed that. The Cowboys needed to show we can have a strong-willed football man, a dictatorial type, as the head coach. They said we did not pay them much; they said we could not work with a coach like [Parcells]. Strategically, this was very important."

In the finer details, Parcells did get the chance to pick his own top assistants, something Jones did not allow in expressed authority to his previous three head coaches, but, contrary to general public assumption, Parcells did not have authority to make draft choices or acquisitions. Jones maintained both roster authority for the Dallas Cowboys and the option of strolling the sideline during games and practices.

"He [Parcells] got decision in the first staff members," Jones says. "After that, draft picks and personnel...the 53-man roster, he did not.

He wanted it, but I would not do that. But, how do I make decisions? With input from the coaches, of course. Never one time has meddling been an issue."

Jones pledged to make the relationship work, saying he would avoid getting careless with the relationship the way he did with Jimmy Johnson, and he found from the start it was for the most part an amicable professional association that functioned better than he ever could have imagined, with one big exception: the team never won the way he thought it would under Parcells. The concept was to increase the talent level, take a step back, and let the coach do his thing. In every way but one, the Parcells experiment was a complete success. That is not to say there were never problems. There were, but they were minor ones, not the debilitating type that plagued Johnson and Jones. Usually, irritations came down to Jones enforcing his authority and Parcells wanting more. A good example comes from the first NFL draft after Parcells was hired in 2003.

With a high first-round choice, Jones wanted, and selected, Terence Newman from Kansas State, widely considered the best defensive back available. Parcells wanted somebody else. In response, he momentarily left Dallas's draft room. You don't want my advice? Fine! Several minutes later, though, Parcells walked back in, announcing he was through pouting and ready to get to work. Jones admired Parcells's honest approach and says he found working with the coach was much easier than expected, so he found himself as relaxed as is possible when a determined man is trying to build a Super Bowl winner. Besides, they did not know it but fortune was beginning to bounce back the Cowboys' way.

Throughout the 2003 draft, Dallas quarterbacks coach Sean Payton joined forces with Dallas scout Jim Hess to adamantly tout a Division I-AA quarterback from Eastern Illinois named Tony Romo. Growing up in Burlington, Wisconsin, Romo was not exactly a high-level recruit as a senior in high school, especially considering he never led his team to a winning record. But as a college junior, he led Division I-AA in passing efficiency, and as a senior he won the Walter Payton Award, given to the top player in all of Division I-AA. Despite his collegiate accomplishments, he went undrafted in 2003. Nobody can say Payton and Hess did not try, though. The two were said to be doing everything but jumping up and down on the chair to get Jones and Cowboys scouting director Lacewell to use a draft selection on Romo that year.

Fortunately for Dallas, Payton is a former Eastern Illinois quarterback himself who had maintained constant contact with Romo throughout the draft, assuring him the Cowboys wanted to sign him as a free agent. Jones did not question the quarterback's talent but says he had little indication anybody else was onto Romo, except maybe the Denver Broncos, since Mike Shanahan, another Eastern Illinois alumnus, was the only other man showing serious interest. Both the Broncos and the Cowboys tried to sign Romo immediately after the draft, but the Cowboys had one major advantage: the team had a desperate need for a new quarterback as it continued to search for an heir to Troy Aikman. So for a $10,000 bonus and the bargain of the decade thus far, Dallas signed free agent quarterback Tony Romo.

From the start of the Parcells regime, appearances were that the strong-willed coach would turn the franchise around, which is all Jones wanted anyway. In a year when longtime Cowboys general manager Tex Schramm passed away and running back Emmitt Smith was released and picked up by the Cardinals, the Cowboys appeared to gain something back on the field. A season-opening loss at home against the Atlanta Falcons (27–13) was troubling but short-lived as the team won seven of its next eight games, charging to the top of the NFC East. A bit of a late-season slide was not enough to diminish a 10–6 season that included a Wild Card playoff game at Carolina. The Cowboys lost 29–10, continuing the franchise's postseason drought dating back to 1996, but Jones and a lot of other observers thought Parcells was just getting started.

The Cowboys acquired high-profile receiver Keyshawn Johnson in the off-season, but Parcells's second season was marred from the beginning when Quincy Carter, the quarterback who led the team to the playoffs in 2003, was abruptly let go for reportedly failing a drug test during training camp. On the surface, this looked like bad news for the Dallas franchise. The team played with 41-year-old Vinny Testaverde at quarterback, and games were often painful to watch as the penalty-plagued team struggled through. The result: six wins, 10 losses. History will show, however, that the year was anything but a loss for the franchise because when Carter was released, it made room on the roster for Romo. Before the start of the season Dallas had acquired quarterbacks Testaverde and Drew Henson. With Carter as the starter, the 53-man squad appeared to have no room for Romo. But all that changed when Carter was let go and Romo became the team's third-string quarterback (he actually scored the winning touchdown on a short run in an exhibition game that year).

In the 2005 off-season, Dallas began to make its most dramatic progress in years in terms of its overall talent level. Using first-round picks to draft Demarcus Ware and Marcus Spears—Parcells was not thrilled about the Ware draft selection—and acquiring Anthony Henry and Jason Ferguson through free agency, Jones and company began to rebuild the team with talent comparable to its championship days a decade before. Generally, Parcells and Jones were in complete agreement about the team's direction in talent, so they had few problems. Debates were more lighthearted than intense. For instance, Parcells preferred the prototypical Big Ten lineman—the bigger but perhaps slower underachiever—while Jones preferred the prototypical SEC lineman—the leaner, faster athlete with potential to dominate when put in the right position. Jones and Parcells also kept more distance from one another day in and day out than was typical with Jones and his previous coaches.

Parcells was both the consummate politician and the ultimate professional, Jones says, and Parcells understood the benefit of proper channels and the meaning of an organizational chart. Parcells had an ear with Stephen Jones, who understood that for the relationship to work, the coach needed a sounding board outside of Jerry. Stephen would listen to Parcells and say no if he disagreed, but if he thought Parcells's argument had merit, Stephen would often take it to his father as intermediary.

Another confidant of Parcells became Rich Dalrymple, the team's director of public relations who joined the franchise from Miami shortly after Jimmy Johnson was hired. Jerry Jones says Dalrymple, like Stephen, was often a sounding board for the coach, acting as a buffer for the owner. Jones says Parcells was uncanny in working the angles, trying to get his way. When the boss said no, it meant no, yet Parcells would try every conceivable play that was above board and fully within accepted professional strategy to persuade him to change his mind.

"He would go to Stephen, Rich...but never behind your back. He would never do that," Jones says. "He would try everything you could imagine to get you to change your mind, but you always knew where he stood.

"Bill was never devious. He would just make you smile all the ways he would try to get around you [in decision making]."

Dynamics of the Dallas team changed the moment Parcells walked into his Valley Ranch office, and Jones liked the transition. Parcells brought intensity to the locker room. Like Jones, he expected to win. Fans, too, expected to win once again. And media from across the country paid more attention to the Cowboys. Every day was the Bill Parcells show, cameras following his every move. Eventually, the focus might have been too much on the coach instead of the team, but for the first couple of years, the Cowboys needed an attention-grabbing catalyst, something to tell fans, media, and the football world that the franchise was serious again about winning.

Details Make a Difference

Having the football team in the hands of a seasoned coach gave the Cowboys and Jones needed stability from the transitional years that followed the historic championships in the 1990s. No more looking around, no more second-guessing. If the team did not win, nobody could say it was because Dallas and Jones did not have a strong enough football coach and personality on board. So Jones let Parcells coach, giving him total control over what transpired on the field and considerable input into roster acquisitions. The influence is evidenced by the fact that many of the Cowboys' new players once played for the head coach in New England or New York, including Keyshawn Johnson, quarterback Drew Bledsoe, and receiver Terry Glenn. A domineering, old-school type who did not like players making headlines if they were not performance related, Parcells cast a large shadow over the Cowboys, but he was also a voice of discipline and reason, something the team needed at the time.

"I was surprised how well it worked," says Jones, referring to having two strong dictatorial types in himself and Parcells. "Pleasantly surprised."

Jones hardly backed away from time with the team in Parcells's presence. If anything, he was as charged as ever, spending time on personnel assessments to try to help the coach get needed tools to win. He was heavily invested in leadership with such a large contract for Parcells and wanted to make sure the talent level gave the Cowboys every possible chance for success. Away from the field, though, the hiring of Parcells gave him more time to focus on the larger picture. Jerry Jones loves the X's and O's of football, but he also loves the pageantry and marketing potential offered by the NFL. Sit with Jones in his office for long and it quickly becomes obvious that he sees the NFL as a unifying cord, able to connect masses of people and communities and enhance quality of life like no other form of entertainment. He views the game as a cross between NCAA football and Hollywood celebrity; an entity where honest competition and creative showmanship go uniquely hand in hand.

"Football is show business," said Jones. "You can't forget it is entertainment. There's a show to put on. If you move away from that, you have wasted great substance."

The unique ability to elicit passion and attention from so many people is what makes the brand so strong, he says. What has kept Jones up at night over the years is making sure the brand is utilized in the best possible ways. That is why, not long after the Cowboys made headlines in the 1990s as being the bad boys of football, the Jones family recognized the franchise had a higher calling. The NFL has long been known for its philanthropy, working closely with the United Way and other compassionate, fund-raising organizations, but Jones wanted Dallas to do something bigger than just tag along.

The family had long been fans of the Salvation Army, believing it to be one of America's most efficiently run charities. Both Jones and his wife, Gene, are on the Salvation Army board of directors, as is their daughter, Charlotte. They are credited with helping develop one of the most effective and creative promotions in the history of the organization.

The Salvation Army is known for its good works, efficiency, and for collecting money in red kettles at shopping centers all over the country during the holiday season. The Jones family recognized that with its traditional Thanksgiving Day game launching the holiday season, the Cowboys had a unique opportunity. With America gathered to watch football, why not kick off the Red Kettle Drive at Texas Stadium? As expected, the Salvation Army loved the idea, recognizing the need for a high-profile national launch. Jones and the Cowboys kicked in almost $1 million to sponsor a halftime show and got the television network to donate eight minutes of on-air time at the half (Charlotte and Jerry met with NBC's Dick Ebersol in New York, getting the unusual commitment; since then, other broadcasting networks have obliged as well). Years later the tradition lives on as Gene and Jerry Jones and the Dallas Cowboys continue to make the charity a top annual priority.

Another family project taking considerable time away from the field will make its public debut in 2009: the Dallas Cowboys' new stadium under construction in Arlington, Texas. The moment Jones bought the Dallas Cowboys, he knew he had to have an eye on a totally renovated or new venue because his 20-year deal with Texas Stadium was ending in 2008. He talked out loud beginning in the mid-1990s about his desire to reconfigure the team's Irving playing facility into a state-of-the-art, interactive, 100,000-seat structure that was unequaled in the NFL. Talking about it was easier than getting it done, however, as politics have a way of impeding progress in professional sports, since tax dollars and complete municipal agreement are almost always required for major stadium construction.

Irving leaders had more than 30 years to assess whether they liked having the Cowboys call the city home, and while a stadium project received plenty of support, more council members than not thought investing millions in a new and improved Texas Stadium was not a good idea. The Irving city council funded an independent study that reported having a professional football team within its municipal confines contributed only $51 million annually to the economy.

"We have had 30 years to measure the impact this team has had on the city," said one Irving city council member. "We've looked at the numbers, and it does not make financial sense."

Never one to let obstacles stand in the way of prudent business, Jones and the Cowboys looked elsewhere. Not having a new stadium was not an option. The team was under pressure to get plans for a new venue under way, and Jones did not want just any stadium or some minor update of the current one. He wanted the Cowboys to play in one of the most visible sports stadiums in the world. So he knocked on nearby Arlington's door, seeing if the city wanted to expand beyond being the home to Major League Baseball's Texas Rangers. Arlington was more than a little interested. Stadium proponents promoted a study, commissioned by the city of Arlington and the Cowboys, that said a new stadium would create $238 million in annual economic impact for the municipality, and a public vote was scheduled in 2004.

With roughly 350,000 residents, Arlington is the seventh largest city in Texas. Lying conveniently along an interstate highway between Dallas and Fort Worth, Arlington is 15 miles from the Cowboys' namesake township, but its accessibility and reputation as an entertainment stop with professional baseball and a popular amusement park drawing visitors made it an attractive site. Besides, negotiations for a new stadium in Dallas had failed. The Cowboys had announced plans for a $650 million stadium at Dallas's Fair Park with $425 million in public dollars to be generated from increased taxes on hotel rooms and rental cars, but the deal fell through when a majority of Dallas County commissioners were not in favor.

With anticipated construction costs soaring into the hundreds of millions of dollars and higher, a municipal partner becomes quite attractive, so Jones and the Cowboys moved to the next viable option. Arlington voters had passed a stadium referendum before. In 1991 they voted in a half-cent sales tax increase to fund the majority of the expense to build a new $191 million ballpark for the Texas Rangers. Research suggested they might do it again, considering the mayor and city council supported the initiative. The vote would not come easy, however, as Arlington in recent years had voted down funding several large projects designed to stimulate the local economy. Residents had rejected building a public transit system, a satellite branch of the Smithsonian Institution, and a development project resembling San Antonio's Riverwalk.

Opponents to building a new stadium for the Cowboys with millions in taxpayer dollars emerged the moment a referendum was scheduled. Calling themselves the No Jones Tax Coalition, members of the opposition raised roughly $45,000 to educate voters on why they thought Arlington's participation was a bad idea. Spending more than $5 million on the other side were Jones and the Dallas Cowboys, arguing that the stadium would boost the economy and be a signature structure that elevated the city's profile. Nobody can deny, said Jones, what the Cowboys' association with Irving did for that city since Texas Stadium was built there three decades earlier. And the stadium he planned to build in Arlington was not just any stadium, but a premier stadium, unlike any structure ever built in the world.

Details of the referendum called for Arlington to increase its sales tax and taxes on hotels, motels, and rental cars, generating $325 million to pay for half of the stadium over 30 years. The Cowboys' requirement was matching the $325 million investment, paying $60 million in rent, and donating $16.5 million for youth sports over 30 years if the referendum passed. The franchise needed approval and time was running out, considering several years would be needed to build the mammoth stadium. Working with a public relations firm, the Cowboys developed a strategy for promoting the vision of the new stadium before the vote.

The public relations strategy did not include Jerry Jones.

The recommendation from the firm was to keep the owner and his image completely out of the public debate so voters could focus on presented facts and information rather than seeing support as some kind of gift to a billionaire owner. The stadium initiative was about

131

community progress and economic development, not Jerry Jones, as objectors argued. But getting Jones to step away was not easy, recalls Rich Dalrymple. He and Stephen Jones had the unenviable task of telling the hands-on owner and general manager he could not be involved publicly in the stadium initiative in any way. Stephen would be the franchise spokesperson; Jerry would be completely out of sight.

"This campaign is 100 percent about how America's Team can help make Arlington America's city," said Rob Allyn, head of the public relations firm handling the vote campaign for the Cowboys. "To make it about personalities really trivializes a very important decision the citizens will make about whether they want to bring the Cowboys to Arlington."

The reasoning made so much sense that Jones obliged, not making one public appearance or uttering one word to the media about the impending vote. Considerable convincing was required before he agreed to step back, however. For better or worse, he had been the face of the Dallas Cowboys since buying the team in 1989. In controversy, he stood before cameras time and time again, just as he stood before the cameras in celebration when the team won three Super Bowls. His trademark as an owner has been taking the shots, facing public situations "like a man." And nobody has the passion for the Cowboys that he does. The stadium vision was his, and who could better articulate that vision than him?

Dalrymple and Stephen are often sounding boards for the owner and general manager, but this task was more difficult. The firm's advice on handling the vote was, well, firm. Research showed the vote needed to be about the stadium, not about the owner. So they took the argument to Jones, strongly advising he step back. In the end, spokespersons for the campaign were former Dallas players Roger Staubach, Troy Aikman, and even Emmitt Smith, playing for the Arizona Cardinals. As Jones feared, the question was asked: where's Jerry?

The Cowboys brand has such allure, though, that Jones's presence or lack thereof did not matter. That and the fact that most of the taxes will be paid by Arlington visitors convinced the majority. The referendum passed with more than 55 percent of the voters in favor. Appearing at the celebratory press conference on behalf of the Cowboys was Stephen Jones, the franchise spokesperson, but not far away was one happy Jerry Jones. With victory in hand, he reemerged, escalating plans from building a nice, state-of-the art NFL stadium to building one of the most dramatic and interactive stadiums in the world. The concept was to imitate in design and structure the enormity of the Dallas Cowboys brand.

"If you extend that to the idea of a venue, the quality of the venue, the size of the venue, it wasn't much of a step to say this must be recognized as one of the best, if not the best, sports venue ever built," says Jones.

Make Them Say "Wow"

Based on Jones's philosophy of learning about an issue before making a decision, Jerry and Gene visited stadiums across the country and throughout the world for several years to get an idea of the type of venue they wanted to build for the Cowboys. They were far more impressed with the large, traditional soccer stadiums found in Europe than anything else. Jones says they toured New York's Bloomberg Tower and Sydney's Opera House, and they went to Paris, Munich, Frankfurt, Amsterdam, and London looking for defining characteristics. They were most impressed by one of the world's signature structures, Wembley Stadium in London; so impressed was Jones, in fact, that he visited there four times. Once, when meeting with project architects, thousands of workers scurried about, easily engulfed by the structure, revealing just how large it was. It reminded him of his first visit to the Houston Astrodome when he was in college and the structure, unique for its time, was new and awe-inspiring. "[The Astrodome] just sucked the air right out of you," recalled Jones.

He said Wembley emanated the same aura in the 21st century that a place like the Astrodome did decades before. "It really gave me some perspective on the task ahead," said Jones. "It helped me in sizing everything up, in terms of capacity and square feet, and really helped me to think at that level, that big."

Texas has a reputation for doing things bigger. Add Jerry Jones to the dimension and, well, you can understand what happened with the Cowboys' New Stadium—naming rights have not yet been decided, though some journalists and Dallas-area residents refer to it under construction as "Jerry World"—between the initial brainstorming sequences and final design. All along, Arlington was getting a modern-day behemoth, but the deeper Jones got into the project, the more spectacular it became. Had Dallas or Irving leaders any idea what features Jones had in mind for the new stadium, they might have pushed harder to make it happen, because the changes made between the initial concepts voters saw in 2004 and the final plans confirmed in 2005 will make the stadium a world showplace for years to come.

Originally costing $650 million, construction costs of the Cowboys' New Stadium soared to more than $1.2 billion by the time Jones and family members got everything in place. Designed by Dallas architectural firm HKS, the stadium is envisioned as a large, unmistakable facility featuring unique, interactive, fan-friendly components. Seating more than 80,000 for football games with the ability to host 100,000 or more for other events, the stadium will feature a 300-foot-tall arch spanning the length of the stadium overhead and anchored on each end deep into the ground.

With shiny glass panels simulating a Dallas Cowboys silver helmet on opening day, a retractable roof that when opened resembles the current trademark hole in Texas Stadium, and 120-foot-tall glass doors on either end that can also be opened or closed depending on weather, fans will have a game-watching experience combining benefits of being amid the live action and pageantry and watching it from the comfort of home. That's because the feature Jones is most excited about is a length-of-the-field, center-hung video board. No looking to end zones to catch replays on undersized screens. The Cowboys' New Stadium will provide fans a bigger picture at eye level than they would get watching the game on a large-screen television in their living room.

On a day before Dallas kicked off its regular season, Jones was delighted when asked about construction progress and expected impact of the stadium, the way a proud parent would dote over a child. He loves stadiums—the good ones, at least. So within seconds of being asked about this project, he walked the 20 or so steps from the soft leather couch where he often sits and meets with visitors to his bulky, slightly cluttered desk, returning with piles of renderings, photos, and information.

"Just wait until you see this!" he said, unveiling one elaborate drawing after another.

Jones demonstrated how fans sitting in the upper decks will be able to look ahead and watch action on a 60-foot-wide flat-screen video board or look down by doing nothing more than shifting their eyes slightly lower to see the action on the field.

"This is all they have to do!" he says, glancing up, then down, up, then down again.

Incidentally, Jones got inspiration for the video board while attending a Celine Dion concert at Caesars Palace in Las Vegas. As the petite singer performed, her presence was made 15 times larger by video screens behind her. The Dallas Cowboys owner, who admits a soft spot for energy and flair, was captivated, if not comfortably confused. "You didn't know what you were seeing," he says, "but you knew it must have been good."

Only the most hardened cynic would not have been impressed with the stadium diagrams and photos, and for Jones, the project is akin to building the ultimate dream home. The Jones family, in fact, has approached the project exactly that way. Each member has been intricately involved. The stadium will have 15 times the space of Texas Stadium devoted to luxury suites, and many will be field level, another special touch of Jones's. (He never understood why all of the highest-paying customers had the highest seats, so he moved many suites down but gave fans in the higher-level seats the giant video board at eye level.) With two times the number of suites the team had to sell at Texas Stadium, the Cowboys should have far more revenue than competitors if they can get them all sold.

"You want the biggest stadium and the highest attendance and the most interest because that can help you score touchdowns, by adding to the value of perception," says Jones.

Gene and Charlotte Jones personally worked on suites in which buyers get more than just a space to watch a game, personally selecting most of the finishing materials and furnishing selections themselves.

Jerry Jones Jr., the franchise's chief marketing officer, is charged with creating an exterior tailgating experience that mimics the best found on college campuses. He visited the University of Mississippi one fall day, for instance, to better understand the aura of the famed Grove, consistently rated as the best tailgating experience in America. And Stephen Jones, in his role as CEO, combed over millions of dollars in construction change orders and approvals. The City of Arlington is locked in at its $325 million contribution and so is the NFL with its $150 contribution, standard whenever a league franchise builds a new stadium, so any extras come directly from Jones's pocket.

"You have to spend to create the 'wow' factor," says Jones. "This stadium is 25 percent more than we could have done to have a nice place for the future of the Dallas Cowboys. But that extra 25 to 30 percent is all of the 'wow.'"

Talking about the construction project in his Valley Ranch office one afternoon, Stephen obviously possesses the same unbridled enthusiasm about the new stadium as his father. He just shows it, in accordance with his personality, in more muted tones. Wearing black cowboy boots that are kicked up on the corner of a desk, with black slacks and dress shirt, he talks about how the family is charged with paying for all of the extravagant details like those found in the luxury suites. They are doing it, he says, because everyone understands the stadium will be the family's lasting signature on the greater Dallas community—if they get it right.

"We just thought, if we are going to do it, why not do it first class?" he says. "For the fans and the community, you've got to deliver. We only get one shot at this. It puts you on an incentive plan. My father will give up lots of money to have people say he did it the right way. We just don't want people to think we messed up.

"It's just one shot. One shot. We talk about that every day. What they say on talk radio during the season, you try not to pay attention to that. But when it comes to something as big and long-lasting as this stadium, it's your reputation at stake and we want to get it right."

Stephen talks about specific purchasing decisions such as bar stools and carpeting being made by his mother and sister, and the irony is not lost on him that it sounds like one big happy home-building project, with an exceptionally high price tag. They are getting close to making the final decisions, and "it feels good," he says, because, "at this point there is just about $50 million left" to sign off on in terms of detailed finishes with the architect. After saying this, he laughs.

"I guess it is like building a very big family house and, oh, by the way, the only time we will use it is for parties 10 or 12 times per year," Stephen Jones said.

For the Jones family, the stadium is a bonding point. During the bleak on-field years following the Super Bowl run the planning kept them "focused and busy." They are all bona fide workaholics. Around the office, each knows his or her role, says Stephen, so they make it work by contributing in their areas of expertise. When the team struggled, they worked together, putting focus and energy on this gargantuan project, creating something for the future. And each family member has ownership in the team and the stadium. That is what Jerry Jones's father did for him and he has done the same for his children, integrating them into the business as stakeholders.

Likewise, Jones worked to make sure the franchise would be secure well into the future. Because Jones so dramatically changed the financial fortunes of his Cowboys since buying the team in 1989, he was able to work an effective financial wonder on the debt structure. Banks were quite willing to take on hundreds of millions of dollars in debt; Jones says he did not have to use his beloved Cowboys as collateral. That meant more than anything else in regard to financing because he did not want to risk the family's precious asset.

"The Cowboys did not guarantee a penny," he said, pleased. "In structuring it, I protected the franchise."

Jones personally pitched in about $75 million in collateral to secure roughly $475 million in financing for a 40-year term at an interest rate just less than 6 percent. Anyone thinking the first Super Bowl is Jerry Jones's biggest coup might need to think again. He has been borrowing money his entire business life and says he would never have dreamed when he moved to Dallas in 1989 such a financing deal would be possible. Consider only that when he first bought the team, banks wanted enough collateral to effectively borrow $2 billion in today's environment. For the stadium, he garnered half a billion for much less collateral than he used to buy the team. Call it the benefit of 20 years of hard work and brand exposure.

"That sizzle helps," he says.

Don't misunderstand, though. While Jones did not have to "dance with the devil" to get his dream stadium built the way he did to buy the franchise, he considers the stakes exceptionally high. In other words, the Cowboys' new stadium has his and his family's constant attention and it is not simply a vanity project.

"I'm hardly cavalier about [almost $500 million in debt]," says Jones. "I know nothing has to stay the same. Boxing went away [from its once-stellar position in the sporting world]. So did horse racing. We did not have NASCAR in those days, and football was not so big. But I think we are building something with staying power because we understand the entertainment value and 'wow' factor. So I feel good about the long-term future of football."

Half a billion dollars, combined with the passion and excitement of overseeing construction of a dream, keeps Jones occupied. Hardly a day has passed since the project began in 2005 that he has not been in a meeting or on the phone talking about the stadium. By 2007, he was making three visits to the site per week, taking visitors ranging from General Electric chairman and CEO Jeff Immelt to Ford and Pepsi executives to see the progress and hear the pitch. The stadium, he says, will epitomize everything he has worked to implement since buying the team in 1989, including the unique sponsor/team associations fans in attendance will immediately notice. In the plaza outside the stadium, the Cowboys will have a Hall of Fame experience—courtesy of a sponsor, of course—while inside the stadium so much sensory stimulation will be going on—courtesy of sponsors, of course—that the game will be like the most popular ride at an invigorating theme park. The image is enough to overwhelm the man who first conjured it up.

"I could not have imagined this coming together like it is," Jones says.

Consider the X-Factor

"You can overdo it, but it is important in looking at personnel decisions to consider the interest and entertainment value."

—*Jerry Jones*

9

Consider the X-Factor

The Dallas Cowboys' 2005 season was the type that can frustrate Jones the most. The team had made steady progress in talent, beefing up the roster with quality players on both sides of the ball, particularly with additions like nose tackle Jason Ferguson and defensive back Anthony Henry. The team was much more competitive than the year before, when everything seemed to fall apart and go wrong that could; when higher hopes were dashed by sloppiness, a lack of intensity, and few big plays. But in Bill Parcells's third season, the Cowboys were solid and competitive, winning nine games and losing seven.

In the NFL, winning seasons do not come easily, so any time a team nudges north of a .500 record, everyone knows they are on the right track. The season was one of could-have-beens, one close loss leading to another, but all the while it felt like the team should be winning. The 2005 Cowboys looked well coached and organized, and on-field discipline was obviously back in force. Quarterback Drew Bledsoe, acquired to take the job from aging Vinny Testaverde, showed promise and poise as the team did in nearly every aspect. Something was clearly and obviously missing, though, and it bothered Jones to the point of action. No more mundane mediocrity for America's Team.

Jones admits in hindsight he probably reacted for several years to feedback from the "bad boys" days when detractors suggested player character mattered less in Dallas than winning, so he worked harder to build a team of agreeable, congenial personalities. He sacrificed instinct that says football is a tough game played by aggressive men and a little bit of rogue independence is not necessarily a bad thing.

"I was getting criticized about the off-field decisions [being sued by the league] at the same time Michael [Irvin] was drawing attention," says Jones. "It was some of the harshest criticism I had experienced.... The pressure was really mounting, taking a toll. They were saying, 'Here's the owner taking on the NFL—he does not follow the rules, why should Irvin? Why should his players?' I consciously said, 'We're going to put more emphasis on good behavior.'"

As the talent level improved, so did the quality of play, but Jones was not seeing the dynamic personalities that had earmarked the Cowboys as America's Team. That does not necessarily mean the Cowboys needed bad boys, just that perhaps they did not have to work so hard to build a roster of choir boys. Jones was seeing in practice how having Parcells on the sideline increased interest in the team. Parcells was a talented coach, but the NFL is full of talented coaches. What made more fans watch Cowboys games was the X-factor, that little something that some people have that makes others sit up and pay attention.

That is exactly what Jones works to bring to the game as owner and general manager. He does not have to be outspoken or host a TV show, but these touches create interest and flair, even if it does come with a little bit of heartache. Fans get closer to the action. They get more involved in the story. The NFL season is long and often monotonous, a series of practices, workouts, interviews, and film reviews. A little spice goes a long way in making an otherwise solid dish more flavorful and interesting, after all. That is why Jones signed controversial defensive back Adam "Pacman" Jones prior to the 2008 season. The media-maligned cornerback was a leader for the Tennessee Titans before his off-the-field legal problems got him suspended for the entire 2007 season. Some pundits wondered if Pacman would ever return to the playing field, but Jerry Jones aggressively pursued the player, signing him in April 2008.

"I'm not dismissing role models," says Jones. "But I have found the 'bad guy' intrigue can help. There's a fine line, but to say you can't have a blemish... A perfect example is Michael Irvin. You don't get that kind of interest he commanded without some controversy and a difference of opinion, and that's off the field, too. When looking at people to join the team, we look first at their giving us a chance to win the Super Bowl, but I also ask for and want to see personalities. I like charisma and star quality, and that can help the team win, too, if they are the right fit."

That is why in the 2006 off-season, following a season that ended in improvement but with few dramatic or memorable moments, Jones went after one of the most talented but maligned receivers in the NFL. Terrell Owens first got Jones's attention as a player for the San Francisco 49ers. Jones watched how the tall, strong receiver moved with the ball in open field after making a catch, and how he captivated the crowd and invigorated his team. Jones also saw how Owens struggled with players and coaches when the ball was not moving his way. Playing in Philadelphia after leaving San Francisco, Owens led the Eagles to a rare Super Bowl appearance but was fighting with Eagles quarterback Donavan McNabb the very next season. Word in many offices around the league was that the player was too much trouble to have, yet Jones had a difference in opinion. When Owens became available, he wanted the receiver.

"I think you have risk in every player that you sign," Jones said after signing Owens. "I wouldn't call this a high-risk move. Not at all."

Cowboys head coach Bill Parcells did not exactly share Jones's enthusiasm, however. By virtue of the coach's contract, Jones held the power to acquire players for the Cowboys. Parcells did not. The owner and general manager consulted the coach about the potential acquisition: Terrell Owens, Dallas Cowboy. The coach was not sold. Parcells wanted more talent to help the Cowboys win, of course, but he was never completely convinced that putting Owens on the squad following his tumultuous tenure with the Eagles, which resulted in destructive team dissension, was the answer. Parcells coached with a dictatorial style, preferring players who quietly and effectively adapted to the system in the same way army privates respond to their sergeant.

Parcells wanted followers and Owens's reputation from his stints in San Francisco and Philadelphia hinted at his being anything but that. Highly sensitive and widely outspoken, Owens had often been his own man in a team game and then some. But Jones had positive experience with players of such accord. Michael Irvin might have contributed to a few off-field headaches, but he and Jones maintained a warm relationship in the years after the receiver retired from football, the result of in-the-trenches bonding between a mentor and player. And Owens's problems were not of a legal nature; his troubles were mostly confined to discontent, as Jones found in checking out the receiver's background. So the Cowboys went after the receiver with the same enthusiasm that led Jones to Deion Sanders.

"Bill was reluctant to really buy into it," recalls Jones. "We had other times he was against something and he would lie in front of the train to try and stop it. This one he did not lie in front of the train, but he did not want to show complete buy-in either. He called it 'the circus.' He also recognized it had the potential to make us a winning team, so he did not try too hard to stop it. So he bought into it in his way. But I'll put it this way: I had to call him and tell him I had done it."

The acquisition created an interesting dynamic for Dallas, teaming the dominant owner with the dictatorial coach and the finicky player, but Jones believed the moment the receiver arrived the union would be good, once the critical adjustment period was over. Parcells, though, was never so sure. Famously, Parcells did not refer to Owens by name on purpose in press conferences, and he did not go overboard to involve him in the team's oft-struggling offense during the first half of the 2006 season. This created angst for Owens, who is convinced, with good reason, that he is one of the NFL's most dominating players when given the opportunity.

The problem, as it turned out, was nothing more than a simple issue of supply and demand. Owens wanted the ball but could not get it with frequency due to the play of Drew Bledsoe, the team's quarterback. Even if the receiver was not featured prominently in the offense, no quarterback could easily miss such an inviting target; Bledsoe, however, was a fraction slower on foot and his throwing arm was not as strong or as quick as it once was. Quickly finding a flashing Owens over the middle was easier said than done, just as it was more difficult to get the payoff pass to Cowboys tight end Jason Witten or receivers like Terry Glenn.

The Cowboys were playing competently in 2006, but regardless of fan-grabbing X-factors like Owens and Parcells, something was still missing. The talent level was up, but the team was still searching for an on-field spark. All signs pointed to the quarterback position. Since Aikman retired, the Cowboys had been in quarterback experimentation mode. The player Jones felt comfortable selling out on never seemed to come available in the draft, and they never found the journeyman with enough oomph left to lead the team beyond a token playoff appearance. The most obvious choice to give the Cowboys a spark was the team's backup quarterback, Tony Romo.

One of the team's most natural, all-around athletes, Romo was a runner-up to Mr. Basketball in high school in Wisconsin and possesses a scratch golf game few amateurs can touch. But he also had up-and-down performances in practices during his three years as a backup. In his first seasons, Romo could dazzle and delight or cause one to cringe with his untamed play. The NFL was increasingly getting away from its prototypical quarterback mentality, but the Ohio Valley Conference it is not. Wild, loose, and carefree was entertaining but potentially dangerous in a league where one turnover is often the difference between winning or losing.

"Once he started playing on the scout team," Jones says, "because he had a lot of impromptu about him, our [first team] defensive coaches would complain because he would be making plays going up and down the field, putting it back across the defense. Our coaches would get frustrated. They would say, 'Stop, we are not playing anybody that does that,' but he would be going up and down the field doing it. You would stop and say, 'Wow.' But then at times it would not work and you would say, 'Why did he throw that ball?'"

Jones and his Cowboys cohorts knew they had a talent in Tony Romo. Newly hired New Orleans head coach Sean Payton, the former Dallas assistant and Eastern Illinois graduate who helped persuade the franchise to sign the quarterback as a free agent in 2003, had tried to talk the team into a trade for Romo. Payton offered to give Dallas a third-round draft pick in exchange for Romo the year before.

Dallas said no. We'll take a second-round draft pick for Tony Romo.

New Orleans said no.

Romo remained a Cowboy.

During training camp of the 2006 season Jones and the Cowboys coaches began to talk seriously about the quarterback's potential contribution, moving him from backup to starter. The team needed a boost, a player to quickly deliver the ball to talented receivers and get the team moving with a full-scope threat, including mobility. The Dallas coaching staff was hopeful but concerned, wondering whether Romo was completely through his necessary apprenticeship and ready to play regularly under the bright lights. They knew if they could just get their quarterback to sit back and pick and choose instead of forcing, the Cowboys might have something.

In his managerial role, Jones was trying to gauge what coaches felt the team had in Romo. He asked Parcells a question: "If you were to draft Romo today, what round would you take him in?" Parcells answered the third round. So they waited, believing Romo was not quite ready, giving Bledsoe another season as a starting quarterback.

Oh, the best-laid plans....

The team was armed with indisputable, Super Bowl-winning talent. Yet the Cowboys looked eerily close in the first half of 2006 as they did throughout the 2005 season when mediocrity barely yielded to winning. Experiments in the NFL are for summer camps and the four preseason games, not the homestretch of the regular season when a franchise is frantically trying to return to its playoff glory days. But in his fourth season, Parcells knew something had to give. In a blowout win at home over the Houston Texans (34–6), Romo got his first NFL regular-season experience, throwing a touchdown to receiver Terrell Owens. The next week the 3–2 Cowboys played at home against the Giants and were losing 12–7 by the half as Bledsoe was sacked four times and threw a crucial interception near the Giants' goal line.

Parcells made the change at the half, pulling Bledsoe in favor of Romo, the former free agent. The Texas Stadium sellout crowd roared in approval, standing in unison and chanting, "Romo, Romo, Romo." His first play in the game was a pass. Romo dropped back and let fly. The ball was tipped by New York defender Michael Strahan and intercepted by Antonio Pearce, and it looked for a split second like Romo might be in for a long season on the sideline. Sports, however, have a wonderful way of offering redemption, and Romo's first failed pass was by no means foretelling of his future. The quarterback completed 14 of 25 passes with two touchdowns and three interceptions. His play was reminiscent of his play in practice the previous three seasons: spectacular at moments and dangerous at others. Parcells saw enough, though, to name Romo the team's starting quarterback the next week.

"Any time you do something like this, it is not without a lot of consideration," Parcells said. "I've been thinking about it for some time. Deep down, I feel like Tony is a different kind of quarterback than Bledsoe, and maybe we might be able to put some of those abilities to work. Maybe we can alter our circumstances for the better."

Parcells had been grooming Romo since they joined the team together in 2003. He had given the quarterback a copy of his "rules to live by" to be a successful quarterback. Romo keeps the list taped to the inside of his locker in Valley Ranch and refers to it before and after each season. They include:

- Ignore other opinions
- Clowns can't run a huddle
- Fat quarterbacks can't avoid the rush
- Know your job cold
- Know your own players
- Be the same guy every day
- Throwing the ball away is a good play
- Learn to manage the game: clock, clock, clock
- Get your team in the end zone

- Don't panic

- Don't be a celebrity quarterback

What happened after the Giants game is a sports phenomenon that often happens to players with imbedded star quality, like Romo. Mistakes made in practice when on the team in a backup role often occur because the player is pressing. When given that top-level blue rating, everything changes. Says Jones, "Once they got blue on them, at any position, but especially a blue quarterback, everything changes. They know they have a chance. They have a different feel for the game. Something happens."

Romo, Dallas's 6'2", 224-pound quarterback, blossomed in a matter of weeks from being a backup player fans cheered for into an All-Pro player who led the Cowboys on an improbable midseason run. Getting his first career start against the Carolina Panthers on NBC's *Sunday Night Football*, Romo led the team to a surprisingly easy 35-14 win on the road. Three weeks later, Romo led the Cowboys over the eventual Super Bowl champion Indianapolis Colts, the NFL's last undefeated team that season. The Cowboys won five of Romo's first six starts and the quarterback quickly became a league favorite, displaying a quick release, an ability to scramble from the pocket and improvise, and an easygoing, aw-shucks smile.

Mexican heritage made Romo an immediate hit with the team's significant Hispanic following, and his gaudy statistics—220 completions on 337 attempts for 2,903 yards and 19 touchdowns in 10 starts—and charm made him an immediate hit with football fans and non-football fans alike. The fit seemed perfect in every way, a Cinderella story revealing that the magic was coming back to Dallas. Shades of glory with legitimate, top-level talent all over the field became a common vision with the Cowboys until the last weeks of the 2006 season. Then the team stumbled as pressure to win down the stretch emerged once again, the type of collapse Jones had come to dread in the decade since the last Super Bowl win.

The Cowboys entered a season-closing, two-game homestand with a 9–5 record and a chance to make a statement. But Dallas lost to Philadelphia (23–7) and to Detroit (39–31) as frustration and finger-pointing began. Fortunately, Parcells was able to regain focus for the Wild Card playoff game at Seattle. The Cowboys played well, fighting back in the fourth quarter, and they appeared ready to win the franchise's first playoff game since 1996 when one of the most heart-breaking plays in recent memory occurred. Romo had led the team down the field in the game's closing minutes. With 1:19 left, Dallas lined up for what appeared to be the short game-winning field goal. Romo was the holder, the only starting quarterback in the NFL to hold on field-goal and extra-point attempts. Parcells, the experienced, Super Bowl–winning coach, should have known better, but Romo was in place as the holder at the beginning of the season when he was just a backup. The change was never made.

The ball was snapped. Romo dropped it, picked it back up, and ran to the Seahawks' 2-yard line before he was tackled short of a first down and a touchdown. Seattle's Shaun Alexander then gained 20 yards on a run, helping to kill the clock and ending the Cowboys' season with another playoff loss. In the locker room after the game, Romo cried. He was inconsolable. He said he never felt so low. Parcells, the legendary coach, did not feel much better. Weeks later Parcells retired, suggesting he could not do it physically or emotionally any longer.

Jones was left holding another season of disappointment. Some franchises may find solace, even joy, at making the playoffs and having an exciting, fan-inspiring run during the season, generating sellout games, headlines, and constant airwave chatter. Not Jerry Jones. He plays the game to win and is not satisfied if the Cowboys are not holding the Lombardi Trophy at the end of the season. In the aftermath of disappointment, with Parcells gone and fresh opportunity to build on a well-established foundation, Jones recognized having a legendary coach was good for both the Cowboys and him.

"Bill Parcells was supposed to be high maintenance," says Jones, "but it was one of the more exciting times we have had because of the attention he drew every time he walked into a room or onto the field.

Well, Bill is high maintenance. But you need in my shoes an appreciation of that value outside of the X's and O's football coach. We did not get that with some of the other coaches."

Jones says the Parcells era went better than he could have imagined in terms of what it did for the franchise and how Parcells worked with him, his family, and the Cowboys organization in the struggle to make the team a winner. Everybody knew Parcells wanted to be king in Dallas, running the team from every aspect down to making draft picks, and those close to the situation say he figured winning would earn more control, the kind he sought. Yet when the team failed to win in the postseason, Parcells was left to ponder his future, and ultimately opted out of head coaching.

Jones looks back at the Parcells era and in almost every area he is pleased with the investment and results, with one big exception. The team never won the way he thought it would. They tried, made some tangible, future-building progress, but in the larger picture—winning Super Bowls—it did not work. When Parcells left Dallas, the franchise had not won a playoff game in more than a decade.

"It didn't register," says Jones of the drought. "One of the biggest surprises I could have gotten. I just never sensed that when Bill Parcells came in we would not have success. We were working so hard. Bill was; we all were. But you look back and say, 'We have not been getting it done.' It gave me a sense of urgency again to take this to the next level."

Embrace Negativity

In the aftermath of the stinging loss to Seattle, Cowboys fans could barely believe what they had witnessed, the team choking away victory in a playoff game. Fortunately, they had just the right forum for hashing, rehashing, and discussing every angle of what was and what could have been until the next season rolled around. The Cowboys organization learned early in Jones's ownership tenure that bad news hurts only when you let it. The Cowboys see critical discussion about the team the way Jones viewed his Texas Stadium lease after he bought the team: it can be an albatross or an asset, depending on how you choose to use it.

Dating back to the days when one bashing headline followed another in Dallas after Jones's arrival in 1989, the team's ticket sales and revenues rose in accordance with controversy, and the franchise had the makings of a case study for handling negativity. "Confront and embrace" is the operative phrase, a kind of "if you can't beat them, join them, then beat them" type of mentality. The year was 2006 and Dallas was coming off a 9–7 season under Parcells in which the Cowboys failed to make the playoffs. Negativity in Dallas was running high, since with a future Hall of Fame coach leading the way, fans expected Dallas to win the way they had a decade before.

Home to hockey, basketball, baseball, football, and several other franchises qualified as bona fide professional, Dallas has been a hotbed of sports talk radio since 1994, just after the Cowboys won their second Super Bowl. The first words spoken by Skip Bayless, the longtime newspaper columnist, on a fledgling AM radio station known as the Ticket 1310 were barely heard by the masses, but it would not be long before every sports fan in the city worth his or her salt knew about the hottest talk radio programming in the region, if not the country. The station came along just as Dallas was making its comeback from the recession-plagued 1980s, and humor was timely, as was over-the-top sports analysis of the Dallas teams. The flamboyant, winning Cowboys were natural fodder for the talk show, and the fledgling station left no joke untold, using male and sports humor as the backbone of its unique programming style. Discussing burps was no more out of order on the Ticket than bashing America's Team or its owner.

When the Cowboys lost their winning ways, the Ticket wasted no opportunity to pontificate on the team's misfortunes. Much as late-night TV talk-show hosts take advantage of opportunity in prime political season, the radio station made fun of coaches, beginning with Barry Switzer and continuing with Dave Campo and Bill Parcells. A highlight became a "Fake Jerry" character who mocked the Dallas team owner and general manager in every conceivable way. The Ticket hosts asked Fake Jerry such audacious questions as whether his son, Jerry Jr., dually served as the team's obnoxious mascot character Rowdy to whether he ever made love to Bill Parcells's "man boobs."

The Ticket did not just bash the Cowboys, of course. They made fun of every leading sports entity in town, and reports were that representatives with the NBA's Mavericks, the NHL's Stars, MLB's Rangers, and even the PGA's Byron Nelson Classic had called the Ticket to complain. The Cowboys, on the other hand, were said to be "calm, cool and, eventually, chuckling cohorts" even though the franchise was getting the worst treatment. Team management considered the dialogue good for community awareness.

Team public relations director Rich Dalrymple made the suggestion to the Joneses when the Cowboys were bidding out services of their new flagship radio station home in the Dallas area in 2006 to make the switch to the Ticket. Only a Dallas-area resident who listened regularly to the Ticket could understand just how audacious a suggestion it was for the Cowboys to move from its comfortable radio home to the most critical station on the radio dial; the station that made fun of the owner and the owner's family and rarely gave the Cowboys a break.

But Dalrymple saw the Ticket, with its fervent audience that placed the station among the strongest in the country in sports talk radio in terms of listeners and demographics, as a can't-miss, synergistic franchise partner. Sure, the station frequently abused Jones and the Cowboys on air, but by becoming a part of the active story lines played out every day and week, the team could only benefit with increased exposure and awareness. The scenario fits completely with Jones's strategy of keeping the game real, but writing the pregame script. In other words, integrity of the game can never be compromised no matter what, but elements surrounding the game must play to the entertainment value.

"They take more frequent and harder shots than the rest of the teams around here, and I really wonder how well the real Jerry takes some of Fake Jerry, especially when it starts getting into the realm of Jerry Jr. as Rowdy," said on-air talent Mike Rhyner, known for his Cowboys negativity, shortly after the deal was announced. "But if we hit nerves, they're savvy enough to not let us know it."

Saying the franchise "got some good advice," Jerry Jones Jr. brokered the radio deal for the Cowboys, allowing the Ticket to keep its trademark negative personalities and programming in place. The agreement called for the station to air unique programming with the Cowboys head coach and also with Jones, who agreed to conduct twice-weekly talk shows live during the season. One minute Fake Jerry was answering absurd questions on air; the next, Real Jerry was on the air giving his insight into next week's game.

Not many NFL owners would tolerate such lack of respect, but that is the thing about Jerry Jones. On one hand, he is known publicly for his ego. Most people assume he would assail those who laugh at his expense. But on the other, he is known privately as a man able to laugh at himself, particularly when he recognizes return. If radio personalities need to pick on him a little to talk more about the Cowboys, he can handle it. Jones and the Cowboys understand the price paid for entering the public realm, and they seek to parlay the dialogue into opportunity.

"We take it all with a grain of salt," says Jerry Jones Jr. "It's not personal. It's all good-natured."

Pieces of the Puzzle

Bill Parcells was gone from Dallas, retired from coaching not long after the Cowboys lost the playoff heartbreaker in Seattle. The game, Parcells suggested, was moving on, but he as a coach was not. Jones was left to find a head coach to meld the Cowboys' talented returning roster, ending once and for all the franchise's Super Bowl–winning drought. He did not buy the team to make money; Jones bought the team to win and win big. With construction on the new stadium under way and the sense of urgency created by the difficult loss, Jones began working harder than he had in years to get the right pieces in place for the Cowboys. The team had talent and winning seemed completely within grasp.

In the weeks following Parcells's departure, Jones methodically talked to a list of qualified potential coaches including Mike Singletary, the Hall of Fame linebacker turned assistant head coach of the San Francisco 49ers; Norv Turner, the two-time NFL head coach and former Cowboys offensive coordinator for two Super Bowl wins who had just completed a season as offensive coordinator of the 49ers; and defensive coordinators Wade Phillips of San Diego and Gary Gibbs of New Orleans. Conventional wisdom among pundits pointed to Turner, a coach Jones likes personally and professionally. Instinct, however, pointed Jones in a different direction.

Jason Garrett was the quarterbacks coach for the Miami Dolphins, just two seasons removed from an NFL career as a backup quarterback. Sitting behind Troy Aikman in Dallas from 1993 to 1999, Garrett impressed Jones during his time as a Cowboy with an unusual under-standing of the game and an ability to articulate offensive philosophy. He was a Princeton graduate, able to serve during his years in a dual role: as a backup to Aikman and as an effective assistant coach, break-ing down defenses and offering finite solutions to scheme challenges. Garrett could play the game, of course, or else he would not have spent more than 10 years as a professional quarterback, throwing for more than 2,000 yards in a backup role that included stints with New York, Tampa Bay, and Miami in addition to his time in Dallas.

In two seasons as quarterback at Princeton, Garrett threw for more than 4,200 yards, earning Ivy League Player of the Year honors as a senior. As a professional, his highlight came during the Cowboys' 1994 Thanksgiving Day game against the Green Bay Packers. With an injured Aikman out, Garrett threw for two touchdowns, leading a comeback win in the Dallas's Super Bowl–winning season. He long before had earned the respect of Jerry Jones, though. Garrett's father, Jim, served as a Dallas scout from 1987 to 2004. That's a key reason Jones moved to sign the backup quarterback in 1993 away from the Canadian Football League. Garrett had pedigree and smarts, key ingredients for a worthy NFL backup.

"You knew immediately he [Garrett] was smart as a whip," says Jones. "He was always clear in communicating and logical in rationale."

Jones had planned to make Garrett a Cowboys assistant coach as his career appeared to wind down in 1999, but the Giants surprised him, adding the backup to their roster for three seasons. Garrett also played in Tampa Bay and Miami in 2004, before becoming the quarter-backs coach of the Dolphins in 2005. "I knew what he had," says Jones, "but he went on and played several more years and we had to wait. He gained much more experience, though, so it worked out for the best."

Although Garrett had coached just two seasons in the NFL, Jones knew with certainty after Parcells departed that he wanted his former player in Dallas in some capacity. The problem was Jones did not know what role Garrett should fill. He interviewed him among the other candidates for the vacant head coaching job but wondered if that was the right role for him. Garrett was seasoned in the league with more than a decade of playing experience and, at 41 years old, was hardly an NFL newbie. But Garrett was just a position coach in Miami without play-calling experience. Dallas had a talented team Jones believed was ready to win big. The Cowboys owner and general manager, with a new $1.2 billion stadium well under way and a serious, unsatisfied hankering to be the best, had "to get the [decision] right."

Rolling the dice with an inexperienced coach, albeit a highly talented one, did not make much sense. Jones felt strongly that Garrett needed to be a Cowboy again, however. So he called Miami Dolphins owner Wayne Huizenga, asking for permission to meet with Garrett. Huizenga agreed that Garrett has serious coaching talent. Getting the big opportunity was just a matter of time, despite his relative coaching inexperience. Understandably, then, Huizenga was not enthused about giving Jones the green light to go after his team's quarterbacks coach.

"[Huizenga] said, 'You can have him if he's going to be play-calling,'" says Jones. "In other words, he could not come to Dallas in a parallel move. He would let him go if it [the job] was a step up."

Huizenga gave Jones 48 hours to see what he could do.

Jones wanted Garrett, badly. But he had a problem. Without a head coach, hiring a coordinator was a highly unusual management move. Who would want the Dallas head coaching job when the offensive coordinator was already in place? Not Norv Turner. In addition, Jones does not believe in "walk-around" coaches, the head man who has neither offensive nor defensive responsibilities, left to walk around practices, looking in on each side of the ball. Jones prefers employees with maximum responsibility. Head coaches, best utilized when dually serving as coordinators, says Jones, are no exception.

Turner was head coach of the Washington Redskins for seven seasons after success as offensive coordinator in Dallas, but he posted a losing career record with just one playoff win and was fired. He was also head coach of the Oakland Raiders for two seasons and was fired by owner Al Davis after compiling a 9–23 record. More than anything, Turner's mark on the game was as an offensive coordinator, a seasoned veteran calm under pressure. Jones hired Garrett, saying he would consider him for the head coaching vacancy but ultimately believed offensive coordinator experience was a necessary first step. With Garrett on board, Turner had no place in Dallas.

"I could not wait to get a head coach," Jones says of hiring Garrett before the head coach was named. "That is the great luxury of being the owner and general manager. I did not have to wait. I can make that call; I can make those trade-offs and not lose my job. I knew the impact on Norv Turner. But it freed me to go and get a defensive-minded coach. He [Garrett] was inexperienced. You did not know what you had until the season. It was just a gut feeling plus the fact that I had little time and had to make the call. Was it undermining the next head coach? Yes. But should you forego great opportunities and let a guy pass like Jason Garrett?"

With Garrett set to call the Cowboys' plays, Jones wanted a defensive coach with NFL head-coaching experience to lead the team. He also wanted the opposite of Parcells, a player's coach over the strong-willed dictator type. When Wade Phillips met with Jones in the owner's Highland Park home in Dallas one cold February morning, he dined on tortilla soup, lobster tacos, and hamburgers. What Phillips gave Jones in return for the nice meal and congeniality was a passionate commitment that showed he badly wanted the job. Leading the Dallas Cowboys to a Super Bowl would be the ultimate crowning for Phillips's long career, he told Jones. Having a talented assistant like Jason Garrett on board was all the better.

When Wade Phillips was hired away from his job as defensive coordinator of the San Diego Chargers at the age of 59 to be the head coach of the Dallas Cowboys, Jones could not have been happier. At the press conference announcing the team's new coach in February,

Jones became emotional, tears welling in his eyes. It was not the first time Jones showed physical signs of emotion as his career as owner and general manager steamrolled toward a milestone 20th year, but it was one of the more publicized. Jones has always been highly charged and emotional, but he asked a friend who is a professional in such matters about his tendency to choke up when doing something in regard to the team, such as announcing a new head coach, getting an answer that confirmed what he already knew.

Since the moment Jones bought the Cowboys, signing papers with his hands shaking over so much debt, enduring the heat for firing Tom Landry, and having to find a way to make the broke team's budget balance, he has been under intense stress. Add to that the passion he has for the team and its players and fans and one can understand why he has so much vested emotion that sometimes bubbles to the surface. The day Jones hired Phillips he was filled with joy because he believed with all his heart the long search—he interviewed 10 coaches for the position, spending more than 90 hours in face time before making the decision—was worth the time and the Cowboys landed just the right man for the job.

Considering the team hadn't won a playoff game in more than a decade and that Wade Phillips had never won a playoff game in two previous head coaching stints in the league, many raised eyebrows at the hire. But what Phillips brought to the Cowboys was something the franchise had not had before under Jones's tenure. Phillips had been a coach in the NFL for more than 30 years and his father, Bum Phillips, had also been a head coach in the league, giving him unequaled experience and knowledge. Known as a player's coach who treats men like men, Phillips, a Texas native who prefers cowboy boots and jeans over slacks and loafers any day, brought an easygoing style buffered by the respect he commands from so many years in the NFL.

For Dallas, the fit with Phillips was even better because the team needed a strong defensive coach who preferred 3-4 schemes. Jones and the Cowboys had invested so much time and money over recent years building the squad through draft picks and instruction to run a 3-4 defense, scrapping it altogether for a 4-3 alignment would have been a significant step backward. The criticism on Parcells's defense was that the team played too soft in its 3-4, rarely blitzing and pressuring the ball. Phillips had been a 3-4 man for many years, but he was regarded as one of the NFL's best defensive coaches because of an aggressive attacking style. Jones hired Phillips as the seventh head coach in Cowboys history under a three-year contract worth $3 million per year.

"We needed to get it right," said Jones. "In my mind, we got it right. This team is best served now, next week, next month, and next season by an NFL head coach with experience, that knows the game, that candidly knows the personnel that are playing the game right now."

Some people were wondering, naturally, if Phillips's hiring was Jones's way of having a softer coach personality in place, but the owner and general manager deflected such talk, suggesting the Cowboys would change nothing operationally between Phillips and Parcells. "When Bill came in," said Jones, "a lot of people didn't think that I would have a strong coach, or deal with a strong personality in making the decisions. The decision-making process around here is the same as it was when Bill was here. When it gets down to it, if we disagree, then I make the call. That's the way it was when Bill was here and the way it's been with any coach we've ever had here."

What Jones did do after Parcells left was go on a mission through draft and acquisitions for strong, athletic players on the offensive line and on the defensive side of the football. Most notably, the Cowboys signed free agent offensive tackle Leonard Davis, the second pick overall in the 2001 draft. Calling this his "most important" and "impacting" free-agent acquisition since Deion Sanders, Jones beat out suitors including the rival Washington Redskins for the 6'6", 366-pound unrestricted free agent. The Cowboys signed Davis to a contract worth more than $49 million, with more than $18 million guaranteed. Paired with such offensive line talent as center Andre Gurode and tackle Flozell Adams, the Cowboys entered the 2007 season with perhaps the most talented line in franchise history.

"The offensive line can be the personality of the team," says Jones. "And we've got a very big, physical offensive line. It is the biggest swing from where we were when Bill left to where we ended up. It's the biggest position swing that I've seen since I've been with the Dallas Cowboys.

"Bill wanted the less athletic ability; the Big Ten and Northeastern type lineman," says Jones. "He said, 'You guys are SEC.' He wanted the underachiever. We wanted the athletes. Leonard's reputation was he had the talent but you could not get it out of him. I felt differently."

Before summer camps began for Dallas in 2007, with a promising young offensive coordinator, a returning All-Pro quarterback, a new head coach known as one of the game's better defensive coordinators, likely the most talented offensive line in football, and more than a dozen other returning players on both sides of the ball considered among the NFL's best, Jerry Jones and the Cowboys had their most promising nucleus since the franchise's Super Bowl seasons of the 1990s.

Heading North

Improved on-field talent is not all that was looking up for Jerry Jones and the Dallas Cowboys in early 2007. The scene around Valley Ranch for some months was reminiscent of the story Jones tells about his college team between his junior and senior seasons; both talented and hardworking, but one year the ball bounced completely wrong; the next year the payoff in suffering came when every bounce went the right way and the team could not lose. For years it was always one step forward, two steps back for Jones and the Cowboys; a roller-coaster ride of criticism and praise, big victories and colossal losses. But something interesting happened to Jones as he began his 19th season of ownership of the Dallas Cowboys. The hard work paid off. The proverbial ball bounced right and he kept coming up a winner, fielding very little criticism and no controversy whatsoever.

In March, Forbes, in its "first-ever proprietary look" at sports general managers, ranked Jones among the top GMs in all of professional sports, including baseball. Forbes ranked Jones higher than general manager Billy Beane of the Oakland A's (the GM profiled in Michael Lewis's best-selling book Moneyball) and 13th among all 98 major sports general managers. Saying its distinctions "will surely raise some eyebrows," article authors Jack Gage and Peter Schwartz wrote, "The success story here is Jerry Jones of the Dallas Cowboys (No. 13), who turned the Cowboys from a has-been to a three-time Super Bowl champion. To his credit, Jones has actually spent less on players, on average, than his league counterparts during his 18-year reign."

The distinction was significant for Jones because although he has been the team's general manager since shortly after buying it, more notoriety comes from his role as owner. But as he matured in the game as both owner and general manager, people were taking more notice. In additional to controlling payroll while increasing the franchise's win-loss ratio, Jones's style, said one owner, was changing the league.

"I think he [Jones] is part of what's best about the NFL and its future," said New England Patriots owner Bob Kraft. "He's...always pushing the envelope for the most creative and fan-friendly things."

Among the more positive off-season moments for Jones came when former Cowboys receiver Michael Irvin was elected to the Pro Football Hall of Fame. In choosing the person to introduce him at the August ceremony, a kind of best man's choice for legendary football players, Irvin asked Jones to do the honors. This might not seem unusual except for the fact that Jones and Irvin dealt with their share of friction while paired together as owner and player throughout the 1990s. Sure, Jones served Irvin in a mentor role and the two were known to be close, but it was never easy. Irvin got in trouble. Irvin complained. Jones tried to get the player to settle down. He hired people to watch the star receiver, trying to keep him on the straight and narrow.

Honors that come from perseverance and patience, of course, are the most rewarding, and for that reason Jones lists being chosen by Irvin to introduce him at the Hall of Fame among his more notable career honors. When Irvin and his wife, Sandi, drove to the Cowboys' Valley Ranch offices in May to see Jones about this special request, the owner could barely control his emotion. But then, neither could the former player.

"Would you..." an emotional Irvin stammered, "could you...be my Hall of Fame presenter?"

Jones was speechless for a moment.

"I was taken aback," says Jones. "When I could get the words out, I finally told him, 'I would be honored.'"

Calling it a highlight of his life—"I can count on one hand the times I've been that happy," he says—Jones became part of a small group of NFL owners to introduce a former player at a Pro Football Hall of Fame ceremony in Canton, Ohio, including Al Davis (Raiders), Art Rooney (Steelers), and Wellington Mara (Giants). To celebrate the momentous occasion, Jones rewarded Irvin by throwing him one of the best parties in Dallas in the summer of 2007, an ultrahip, no-expense-spared sports celebrity gathering. Held in the Ghostbar of the new W Hotel in Dallas, the party featured former and current Cowboys players, Cowboys cheerleaders dancing go-go style, and flat-screen televisions replaying highlights of Irvin's best years with the team.

Life for Jerry Jones was getting really good; it was as if almost two decades of stress and hard work were paying off all at once. He was talking about working harder than ever before, doing more appointments and more selling and marketing, but he was also smiling more and enjoying the ride more than at any time before.

When NFL owners convened in Nashville in late May, just one week after Irvin asked Jones for the introduction, to decide the host of the 2011 Super Bowl, Jones and company felt they had a winning bid for North Texas and the Cowboys' new stadium in Arlington. With 20,000-plus more seats available for the game than competing bidders and with the Jones and Cowboys marketing muscle behind it, NFL owners had a compelling reason to give North Texas the nod over Indianapolis and Arizona. Former Cowboys Hall of Fame quarterback Roger Staubach served as lead pitchman for Jones, telling the league's 32 owners in a closed-door session how the extra revenue and flash of the new stadium would give the NFL a rare opportunity. The owners' vote was close, requiring four ballots to narrow the competing field, but the final tally was 17 votes in favor of Arlington, 15 votes in favor of Indianapolis.

"We [Detroit] had just hosted the Super Bowl the year before," said Bill Ford Jr., whose family owns the Detroit Lions, "so I knew what a huge undertaking that is. In my mind he [Jones] was a difference. Part of my thinking in supporting the Dallas bid was Jerry's capability. He's not going to allow anything but a first-class Super Bowl in Dallas. That is the only way he will do it."

The vote was a ringing endorsement for Jones and the Cowboys, who endured several years of political heat over trying to build the new stadium in the metro area. Dallas was not interested as a planned deal fell through to build a new venue in Fair Park, and Irving was not interested in replacing Texas Stadium. When the league awarded the North Texas contingent the 2011 Super Bowl, Arlington leaders and voters looked awfully smart. Jones had already landed the Cotton Bowl and the Big 12 conference championship game annually for the stadium. Talks were also under way to host a game every year between Jones's alma mater, Arkansas, and its former Southwest Conference rival, Texas A&M, but no event in sports compares with the Super Bowl, expected to bring more than a quarter-million visitors to the Dallas area in February 2011. The region has never hosted a Super Bowl before, so for Jones, landing the big game was the next best thing to winning one.

In honor of Dallas's winning bid, *Sports Illustrated* ran a large feature article on Jones and the new stadium under the headline, "The King of Texas." In the article, writer Richard Hoffer calls the owner "a ball of energy at 64" and "impossibly charming." What a long way Jones has come from the day he got blasted in *The Dallas Morning News* for being "annoying" and always saying "the wrong thing." But if all that were not enough, *Forbes* honored Jones and his team once again by announcing just as a new NFL season was about to begin that the Dallas Cowboys had become the most valuable sports franchise in the world—worth more than the New York Yankees or the Washington Redskins—at $1.5 billion.

"When *Forbes* says the Dallas cowboys are worth $1.5 billion," says Jones, talking to a visitor in his office days after the magazine made the announcement, "even if they are low—and I think they are—it makes the game bigger, it makes it seem more important and valuable. When the team takes the field, as a result, the needle of interest moves up.... People see the Dallas Cowboys...the most valuable team in America."

Not that it matters, Jones continues, but in his opinion the magazine did underestimate the team's value. Detailing why, one realizes he has a point. The *Forbes* calculations took the team's new stadium into account but not the fact that the team manages its own merchandise and licensing, which no other team does. The Cowboys are one of the most recognized brands in the world, selling more licensed jerseys, T-shirts, and the like than any other franchise. When the Cowboys win, the franchise reaps millions, and without those numbers *Forbes* cannot put a price on the franchise's value. Suffice to say, Jones concludes, the $1.5 billion assigned value of the Dallas Cowboys is low. Very low, especially if the Cowboys win another Super Bowl any time soon.

"They missed the mark," Jones says. "When we won the first Super Bowl in 1993 I was asked what it was worth to the franchise and I said $50 million. I was wrong. It was worth $200 million. If you want to work it—*if* you want to work at it—it would be worth $300 million today, but that's from handling your own merchandise, the stadium, and licensing. If you are growing the pie, it can be made into that kind of value.

"But [the ranking] means something," says Jones, and he is not talking about validation for his risking most of the family's net worth in buying a money-losing football team in 1989. "It's valuable because it puts more shine on the franchise and the players and elevates expectations of everyone involved."

The moment was not lost on Jones, though, as he could not help but reflect on changes with his franchise over the years in regard to some others in the NFL and even in other professional sports. Values such as the *Forbes* ranking, he says, are worthless if you do not put them to work for you, but most people "would be surprised that many of the owners do not want to hear it."

"They just want to play the game Sunday and split the television money," says Jones. "But television would not pay any big rights fees if our teams were valued at $10 million. That's why it means something."

Jones was not surprised the proverbial pendulum of momentum was swinging his way, but he did find himself uncharacteristically at a loss for words when asked about it. When the Dallas team was not winning, the franchise never stopped working, so it only made sense that after a while good things would happen recognition-wise in bunches.

"We have been spreading the kerosene," said Stephen Jones, providing an apt answer for his father.

Stephen recounted how in the quieter times—the years after the Super Bowl run—they focused on the backbone of the business so the rest would flourish when the team won big again. He said winning early in ownership was good for the family, "a great blessing" because they learned a lot and built the infrastructure afterward. "If we get into those runs again, we're prepared for it," he said.

Flanked by his wife and their teenage daughter and preteen son, Stephen Jones looks to the future with the same forward vision as his father.

"Now we need a match," he said. "The match is winning."

Taking Ownership

"I don't have all the answers.
Sometimes it [managing the
team] is like holding Jell-O."

—*Jerry Jones*

10

Taking Ownership

For a journalist covering the beat of a professional football team like the Dallas Cowboys, the key to success is to learn how to gather valuable and useable information throughout the days, weeks, and months on the job outside of the regularly staged press conferences. See the head coach, an assistant coach, or the team's general manager standing alone in a rare moment and strike up friendly conversation about anything from the weather outside to last night's dinner guests to a play the previous week. Then, the journalist goes for the kill, turning the conversation to a specific, team-related subject for response or information other journalists do not have.

Thus, it's not surprising that Jean-Jacques Taylor's most memorable story from hundreds filed over several years as a writer for *The Dallas Morning News* comes not from a regular press conference but from a happenstance dinner, in his first months on the job, with Dallas Cowboys owner Jerry Jones. The married, 40-year-old sports reporter—who did not play football as a student at Ohio State University but is known to engage in the sport for hours on end via a video game and large-screen television—was at an NFL owners meeting in San Diego, California, in 1995, barely into a new assignment as Cowboys beat writer. Team owner and general manager Jerry Jones was in the midst of searching for a new coach for his Super Bowl championship team.

The Barry Switzer era with the Cowboys had ended, predictably, and speculation in the press and among fans was rampant about whom Jones would interview for the vacancy. Without a press conference to attend and in need of unique information, Taylor stood near the elevator in the San Diego hotel where NFL meetings were being held for several hours, waiting for Dallas's owner and general manager to appear, at which point he could be courteously accosted for questioning. Standing and talking to Dallas scouting director Larry Lacewell while he waited, Taylor turned at the sound of an elevator door opening to see Jones and Kansas City Chiefs owner Lamar Hunt emerge together.

Looking for a scoop, Taylor went in for the journalistic kill.

Do you have a moment to talk about the coaching vacancy? Taylor asked.

Not really, said Jones. I'm on my way to a meeting. The only way to talk is to come along.

Having no wallet, no money, and no idea of where he was going or how he would return to the hotel, Taylor grasped the opportunity, filing into a limousine waiting outside the hotel with Jones, Hunt, and Lacewell. He listened for 30 minutes as Jones and Hunt talked on the way to the airport, where the Chiefs owner was dropped off. Now, said Jones, you are heading to dinner with my family at a restaurant on Coronado Island (an exclusive community just off San Diego's coastline).

If you have any questions, Jones said, now is your time.

During the remaining 20-minute ride, Taylor learned that the Dallas owner and general manager planned to interview NFL coaches George Seifert and Sherman Lewis for the open head coaching job. All information reported in the media prior to Jones's confirmation of prospects had been speculation, so the journalist had just effectively scooped the competition. At the dinner table, Taylor sat with the Jones family and Lacewell, excusing himself after the appetizer was served and consumed to make a phone call to *The Dallas Morning News* newsroom, dictating the story for the next day's edition. While the journalistic coup was on its way through editing and typesetting, Taylor enjoyed dinner with his hosts, sharing at the end a 114-year-old port purchased by Jones. After dinner, Taylor and Lacewell rode back to the hotel in Jones's limousine.

When new Dallas Cowboys head coach Wade Phillips, hired by Jones following the retirement of Bill Parcells, was scheduled to make his first appearance before the opening of Dallas's 2007 training camp in San Antonio, dozens of journalists, including Taylor, filled available seats and standing room around a small stage to hear what he had to say. The white tent that shielded the stage and was erected on the plaza surrounding San Antonio's Alamodome baked in the Texas summer sun.

Seated in the front row, Taylor and his journalistic colleagues anticipated what Phillips might have to say about inheriting a 9–7 playoff team that would be returning 21 of 22 starters, including All-Pro quarterback Tony Romo, who had the talent to roll from the pocket and successfully strike a target on the run, and wide receiver Terrell Owens, who might be the best ball-catching runner in the NFL. At a quarter past the scheduled 3:00 PM start, Dallas owner and general manager Jerry Jones, wearing a striped Cowboys logo polo shirt, strolled into the crowded room. Jones was accompanied by his oldest son, Stephen, the team's CEO; head coach Wade Phillips; and a well-suited gentleman unidentifiable to most in the audience. Since the press conference signaled the start of a new year, Jones provided opening remarks.

We are glad to be in San Antonio for training camp, said Jones.

The time is historically important, he said, because this is the first-ever NFL training camp to have a title sponsor.

Welcome to Dallas's Ford Tough Training Camp 2007.

Backed by Ford Motor Company through a multiyear, multimillion-dollar deal made exclusively with Jones and the Cowboys in promotion of the company's best-selling Ford F-150 pickup trucks, the training camp, with practices open free to the public and expected to draw more than 150,000 fans in all, featured interactive fan activities, live music, and concessions. On the same day in Allen Park, Michigan, the NFL's Detroit Lions opened training camp with no title sponsor, very little fanfare, and a press conference focused on the words of the head coach. Two days later, similar scenes took place in Jackson, Mississippi (New Orleans Saints); Nashville, Tennessee (Tennessee Titans); and Flowery Branch, Georgia (Atlanta Falcons). In San Antonio, Texas, however, Dallas Cowboys owner and general manager Jerry Jones was on a mission and it did not exactly coincide with the mission of dozens of reporters in attendance, all of whom were waiting to hear about prospects for the upcoming training camp and season.

"This," said Jones, clasping tightly to the spotlight, "is the most significant contribution Ford has ever made to any team. I want to introduce Dave Mondragon, Ford's southwest market general manager, to tell you about this because it is a big deal for us."

As Phillips sat on the stage, occasionally wiping sweat from his forehead while patiently waiting his turn to address the media, Mondragon talked about Ford and its partnership with the Dallas Cowboys for more than seven minutes. Yes, combining Jones's introduction, that was a 15-minute infomercial for America's second-largest automaker, Ford Motor Company, which just opened the training camp press conference of a football team. One in the audience expected the first question from the throng of journalists in attendance to be along the lines of, "Coach Phillips, what kind of car do you drive?"

Instead, Phillips continued to wait as the stage lead moved from Jones to Mondragon and back to Jones. When the Cowboys owner and general manager finally talked about the team, it was as if he knew the eyes of Texas were on him, with representatives from dozens of daily newspapers and television stations from Houston to San Antonio to Austin and Dallas gathered in the warm, cramped quarters.

Fans are going to love this team, he said.

We have the best coach, he said.

Our tackles are much improved, he said.

Our quarterback has so much promise, he said.

More than 20 minutes into the press conference, after explaining the importance of a training camp sponsor, yielding the floor to the title sponsor's representative, and running down strengths of the team position by position, Jones finally turned the microphone over to Wade Phillips, the new head coach of the Dallas Cowboys.

"Hearing all those good things," Phillips said, "it sounds like we should win them all."

Journalists laughed collectively.

One individual sitting in the back row turned to another, mumbling audibly, "He'd better!"

The Cowboys may have the America's Team moniker, but the franchise, in the truest sense, belongs specifically to the Jones family and Jones, who holds both ownership and management control. Franchise popularity, judging by ticket and merchandise sales, may be at an all-time high almost two decades after the oilman bought the football team, but achievement and discourse starts solely with one.

"I bought this team to run it," says Jones.

Run it, he does.

And should Jones apologize? Most owners are not so visible, but he is not the first football general manager to be directly involved. "Tex Schramm taught me that," said Jones. "I read his book, so to speak, though I have added many of my own chapters. But I did not invent this. I'm not the first GM to do it."

A less-voiced opinion is that few qualities can humble and get the attention of a man like losing. When Jones bought the Cowboys and immediately suffered through a miserable one-win season, he and the organization worked overtime to quickly get to the top. In recent years, they have worked hard building a firm, multidimensional franchise foundation, doing everything they could possibly do to win, but hope and optimism often shielded reality.

"In the NFL, before the season, all teams think they are good," said Stephen. "You think, *If we could just have this player come through or that player come through, we have a chance.* But usually it does not turn out that way. If you don't have the players at each position, you are not going to win big."

In the quieter years that followed the historic Super Bowl run, Jones and the Cowboys tinkered a bit and learned, figuring out what worked and what didn't. Football fans watching Dallas may have thought somebody was asleep at the wheel as the proud Cowboys slumbered along in what one could only label as subpar play at best, but because the team won early in the ownership's tenure and served some humbling lessons afterward, Jones and the Cowboys organization knew better what to build on. By 2007, efforts were showing in a big and visible way.

"In the late 1990s, we were optimistic. You think, *Maybe this year*," said Stephen. "But we learned a lot and did something about it. Starting four to five years ago, we began putting the players in place to build it back up, like DeMarcus Ware. Is he going to come through? Yes. Is Terrell Owens going to come through? Is [Jason] Witten going to come through? [Anthony] Henry? Yes, yes, yes."

With a firm dose of several years' worth of humility, a decidedly more talented team, and other pieces in place they had been striving for years to assemble, Jerry Jones and the Dallas Cowboys were back as one of the best and most interesting teams to watch in the NFL. "When you've won, you want to win again," says Jones. "It's the number one thing that motivates me."

A New Season

The first game day of a new year had arrived. Jerry Jones lives for these moments. He enjoys an evening at the beach, a morning bird hunt, big family holiday gatherings, and even football practices, but he cherishes and adores game day, particularly when his beloved Cowboys are open-ing a new season of promise at home. In early September 2007, the division rival New York Giants were visiting, providing a first barom-eter of his team's touted off-season progress, which included coaching changes, offensive line additions, and defensive lineup maneuvering. The preseason showed particular promise, with the offense easily mov-ing the ball downfield behind well-protected starting quarterback Tony Romo and a collection of seasoned, superlative receivers including Terrell Owens and tight end Jason Witten.

Jones awoke the morning of opening day 2007 in the comfortable confines of his Turtle Creek home in the upscale Dallas neighborhood with a warm cup of coffee in one hand and page one of *The Dallas Morning News* in another. Most billionaires and professional sports team owners might suggest they don't read stories about themselves or their enterprise, but Jones will not. He pays acute attention to the media, particularly what is written about the Cowboys. Jones knows from experience you cannot trust your own headlines, especially the positive ones, but he values the feedback much as a restaurant owner combs over reviews.

If they are talking about you, you had better know what they are saying!

On the day at hand, headlines went down smoothly. A full-color picture showed Jones in front of his three Super Bowl trophies under the headline "Stars in His Eyes." A lengthy feature story told of Jones's ascension from renegade rookie to respected leader in the NFL. All barometers for the franchise were pointing upward, reflecting years of hard work and determination to win. Jones relished the moment, but instead of finding personal glee, he felt personal pressure. For him, that meant beating the New York Giants on opening day and ending the season with another Super Bowl win.

Kickoff was not until 7:00 PM because NBC was in town, with its prime-time cameras and hosts Al Michaels and John Madden, making Dallas and Texas Stadium the featured event of the new NFL season. Most of the league's 32 teams had already played. The Cowboys had season-opening network cachet, thanks to the tradition-laden Blue Star and personalities like Romo, Owens, and Jones. The Dallas Cowboys owner and general manager arrived at the stadium in the early afternoon even though kickoff was hours away. Jones generally likes to arrive early, walking through the stadium, seeing everything from concession stands to the television network setup. If he were a retail store manager, like his father was years before, it would be like arriving early to work the morning before Thanksgiving Day. To properly serve customers and have a big business day, he needs to know exactly what is going on from every angle. Plus, the owner and general manager has obvious nervous energy, fueled in part by enthusiasm from an opportunity to win and in part by a fear of losing.

"I like to get here at least three hours early on game days," he says. "Bigger games, I get here even earlier."

Roger Goodell, the second-year NFL commissioner chosen by Jones and his comrades to lead the league into the early 21st century, was there, visiting with Jones in his 50-yard-line suite, which sits just above the Bob Lilly sign on the Ring of Honor that surrounds the interior of Texas Stadium. Opening day 2007 was busy in the NFL. The New England Patriots were accused of spying on the visiting New York Jets by stealing signals via videotaping, and, far worse, a player for the Buffalo Bills, Kevin Everett, suffered a spinal cord injury. Early reports had suggested complete paralysis for Everett. Goodell could not keep his eyes off television screens flashing in the suite with periodic updates. He left twice for telephone updates. In between, though, he talked about Jones and the impact the Dallas owner has had in his nearly two decades in the league. Goodell served as assistant commissioner under Tagliabue, traveling considerably with Jones in his role as director of overseas development. So he knows well the story of Jones and his Dallas Cowboys and their impact on American professional football.

Jones rewrote the league's charter, showing, perhaps a bit ahead of its time, how teams could develop additional licensing revenue, Goodell said.

Jones understands marketing like few others in sports and has much to offer fellow owners willing to listen, Goodell said.

Jones will one day be remembered for his considerable impact on the game, Goodell said.

On the day at hand, all Jones wanted to do was beat the Giants, since, on game days, he measures his contribution to the franchise one victory at a time.

"I hope we win," Jones said, before adding, "I think we will."

Less than 30 minutes remained before kickoff, and Jones scampered from the family's suite down the stairs to the concourse that traverses Texas Stadium. He made the dash across the crowded space as fans, waiting in line for bathrooms and concession stands or trying simply to reach their seats amid the mob, shouted encouragement to the owner. Seconds later, Jones was bounding down the steps that lead to Texas Stadium's field level. There, he shook one hand after another, greeting sponsors and their family members and guests. With the exception of Gene, the Jones family was on the field, meeting and greeting, smiling and taking pictures. Charlotte was wearing heeled boots and a big smile, managing the pregame entertainment and greeting guests simultaneously; Jerry Jr. was talking to the owner of a favorite restaurant about what he recently ordered on a visit; and Stephen was shaking hands, thanking everyone for coming to the game.

Back in the suite, Gene tended to guests, including Mr. and Mrs. Ross Perot, Mr. and Mrs. Pat Summerall, and Linda Michaels, whose husband, Al, was about to go live on the air with play-by-play for NBC. Of all the stops Linda Michaels made during the season, she said Dallas was among her favorites because Jerry and Gene are such gracious hosts.

At kickoff, Jones was back from the field and in the suite. Also there was Everson Walls, the former Cowboys defensive back Jones once released, and Ron Springs, the former Cowboys running back. Springs is in a wheelchair. He and Walls were honored on the field before the game as the game's special guests. Springs needed a kidney transplant and his former teammate, Walls, donated his. "That's a story right there," Jones said. "That's a teammate."

Air has a way of standing still in Texas Stadium, and on that muggy night it was unusually motionless. The crowd was unfazed, though, on its feet and making noise, and Jones was energized, reaching toward the crowd with a clenched fist. If Jones were on a heart monitor, his would undoubtedly be racing. One could almost see his veins pulsing with intensity.

Goodell had some good words about you, he was told.

Jones uncharacteristically did not respond. His eyes were glued to the field. Everything he did professionally in the off-season was built around this, the game. Normally Jones would be long gone by now, watching with Stephen and Jerry Jr. in his minisuite in the end zone. There, he can watch the game uninterrupted and without showing nerves and stress to his guests. If he wants to curse and show frustration, he can. If he wants to watch a replay several times, he can. But with Goodell and other special guests on hand, he remained in this suite beyond the game's start.

When his teenage granddaughter stood in the aisle on the game's first play, innocently obstructing the view, Jones gave her a quick tap on the shoulder and a silent hand signal to sit down. He's never long on patience but especially not when the Cowboys are playing. Jones remained in the family's suite until just after the Giants' third offensive play of the game, when quarterback Eli Manning found receiver Plaxico Burress on a 60-yard scoring pass.

Poof, just like that, Jones was gone, hurrying from his crowded 50-yard-line suite to the smaller end zone suite to watch the game with his sons. Had he hung around, Jones would have seen much of the group (minus Perot, who was too far away on the suite's front row to get a glimpse) watch a new Papa John's pizza commercial with amusement. The commercial showed Jones break dancing in hyperspeed, flips and all, while addressing his team in the locker room. The spot is a ruse, of course, animation at work, depicting the owner doing dance moves he could never do in reality. What it shows, though, is just how far the impact of Jones and the Cowboys goes in Dallas and throughout the NFL. One minute he's on the field greeting sponsors as a host; the next he's talking to NFL commissioner Roger Goodell as an owner; the next he's off to watch the game in solace so he can effectively assess the Cowboys' on-field talent as a general manger; and the next he's lending his celebrity to a pizza commercial.

Fortunately, the game's beginning was not an indication of the regular season to come. The Cowboys struggled here and there defensively against the Giants as Manning passed for more than 300 yards, but with an injured Michael Strahan, a strong Cowboys front, and talented skill-position players, the Giants defense was no match for Tony Romo and company. Dallas took a 17–6 lead just before the half when Romo found Witten for a score, and Jones, back in the family's suite, was celebrating. Jones hugged and high-fived everybody in sight, and his daughter, Charlotte, standing nearby, hit her father with three celebratory rabbit punches to the abdomen. Before the night ended, Romo had passed for 345 yards and four touchdowns as the Cowboys scored seemingly at will and beat the Giants 45–35. The outcome was a hint of what was to come. When the Cowboys returned home for a late-September contest with the Rams, the team was undefeated and the league as a whole and fans everywhere were paying close attention.

Benefits of Alignment

By the time the St. Louis Rams visited for a game on September 30, the Cowboys had emerged as a team to beat in the NFC. The offense was hitting on every possible cylinder. All the pieces Jones and the Cowboys put in place in the previous few years were making a difference, including Terrell Owens, the offensive line, and running back Marion Barber, but there is no denying Tony Romo was the spark that lit the fire. He has a quick release, unusual mobility, and a knack for making big plays. Sure, Witten was one of the best tight ends in the game and an easy target for any quarterback to hit, but Romo seemed to have that something extra that made Dallas go.

Roger Staubach had it. Troy Aikman had it. And so does Romo. It's not just on the field that he excels, either. During the off-season, Romo spent his time playing golf—he's a zero handicap amateur golfer—dating celebrities, including country music singer Carrie Underwood, and making frequent appearances on radio talk shows. With an easygoing smile and a carefree spirit, fans warmed easily to the player with the magical, two-syllable name—RO-MO. Neither did it hurt that Romo is a third-generation Mexican American—his grandfather, Ramiro Romo Sr., emigrated from Mexico to San Antonio, Texas, as a child—and Dallas has the largest Hispanic following of any NFL team, translating into millions of dollars in merchandise sales for the franchise. (No. 9 Cowboys jerseys were completely sold out at many retail outlets throughout the 2007 season.)

With the Cowboys off to a 3–0 start, Romo seemed charmed in every way, throwing touchdowns and smiling easily afterward, but Jones had not yet signed him to a new contract with the team. In the last year of a four-year deal, Romo was making roughly $1.5 million in salary, but he had already earned a new, multimillion-dollar contract by virtue of his emerging stardom and spectacular play. Pundits were wondering whether Jerry Jones had lost his mind in not already having brokered a new deal with his budding star quarterback. Jones, however, wanted to hedge his bets. He loved Romo and thought he was perfect for the Cowboys, but he was not sure a half season was enough to judge whether the quarterback was worth being paid as one of the NFL's best.

The difference over several years could be millions of dollars, and Jones learned from experience how one contract can ruin a team's salary cap position. So the owner and general manager watched and waited during the early part of the season for more convincing signs of Romo's worth.

With veteran defensive end Greg Ellis, Jones had no time. One of the franchise's most talented and reliable defenders for years, Ellis is perhaps best known for being taken by the Cowboys ahead of Randy Moss in the draft. A regular starter and the Cowboys' representative with the players' union, Ellis is vital to overall team chemistry because his happiness sets the tone and defensive effectiveness. When healthy, he's known as an imposing pass rusher, able to beat slower tackles with superior quickness.

An Achilles tendon injury from the year before kept Ellis out of the Cowboys' first games. He was making $2.5 million a year but had an injury insurance policy issue that made retirement a legitimate option. Ellis's salary was guaranteed the minute he made the team, and his insurance policy allowed him to play four games upon return from injury before making a crucial decision: retire and collect the insurance money for suffering a career-ending injury, or keep playing beyond the four games, forfeiting all claims on the insurance money. To get Ellis back on the field and to solidify the team's morale, Jones had his own decision to make: restructure Ellis's deal, spending more money, or take the savings and let Ellis decide on his own what he wanted to do. Ellis's concern was no secret in Valley Ranch and beyond. The player wondered aloud what the owner was going to do, and he was letting the insurance issue keep him on the sideline.

Jones did not have to do anything, yet he had a lot invested in Ellis over the years and the Cowboys needed his talent and presence. So on the Saturday morning before the Rams game, Jones went to work. Upon finishing his daily exercise routine, Jones went personally to Ellis's home, meeting with the player to hammer out details of a new contract. For Ellis to be eligible for the Rams game the next day, the deal had to be completed by 3:00 PM, according to league rules. Working to beat the clock, they made final agreements at roughly

2:59 PM, allowing Ellis to make his on-field debut for the Cowboys against the Rams. The deal gave Ellis a raise of more than $500,000 per year, allowing the player to return to the field, walking away from the injury insurance policy. When they shook hands to seal the deal, the player jokingly promised six sacks against the Rams. He got one, showing he remained a prominent factor on the field. In his suite watching the game, Jones celebrated as Ellis took the Rams' quarterback down and Texas Stadium fans stood in approval.

"I was hugging him in my mind," Jones said. "I just knew he was going to get one today."

Jones, Ellis said, proved he would not throw the player away "like trash" and showed him "some love." The move also showed Jones was willing to spare no expense in giving the team the ammunition it needed to win. Weeks before, the Cowboys had signed defensive lineman Tank Johnson, the former stalwart Chicago Bears player serving a league suspension over a weapons charge (recall Jones's decision that he would not punish a player for blemishes on his record). With the defense solidified from a contract and talent perspective, more attention turned to the offense, Romo in particular. And when the St. Louis Rams visited Texas Stadium, Jones and Cowboys fans got a glimpse of what they had been looking for late in the second quarter.

The Cowboys were mired in a 7–7 tie and playing sluggishly. They had the ball at midfield, facing third down and short yardage. The crowd was totally out of the game, barely making a peep. Romo was in a shotgun formation and center Andre Gurode snapped the ball high and over his head. With the Rams defense in active pursuit and the live ball rolling around on the ground toward the wrong goal line, Romo chased after the ball, kicking it further backward before finally scooping it up on the Cowboys' own 17-yard line.

Don't give up a touchdown, Romo recalled thinking to himself. *Don't get killed.*

With the ball in hand more than 25 yards away from the line of scrimmage, Romo could have easily thrown it away, avoiding a costly sack and letting the Cowboys punt on the following down. Logically, he should have thrown it away, yet Romo followed his instinct, turning upfield. He avoided Rams linebacker Raonall Smith, and with running back Marion Barber blocking, he continued making progress up the field. When Romo appeared to be stopped short of the first down, he paused and pump faked to throw off a defender before continuing the run. He got the first down, barely, and the Texas Stadium crowd rose to its feet, rubbing its eyes.

Was that Roger Staubach?

After the play, Romo was laughing with Terrell Owens, saying he was going to be on blooper reels. Five snaps later, Dallas scored as Romo dashed in for a rushing touchdown, emphatically spiking the ball, and the team never looked back, convincingly beating the Rams 35–7. The play was identified in the Dallas media as a career-defining moment for the quarterback. *The Dallas Morning News* ran a full-page, six-photo spread documenting the dramatic sequences, and his play made highlight reels on almost every sports show. The quarterback's head-turning play—Romo also passed for 339 yards and three touchdowns in the game—was garnering attention throughout the league, including that of Jones, yet the owner and general manager was not ready to make a deal for the type of money Romo's agent was asking. The one play was dramatic, yes, just as Romo's play had been all year, but Jones did not yet have all the information he was looking for to make a decision. Millions of dollars and the team's future were at stake, after all.

Several days after the Rams game, as the Cowboys were preparing to travel to Buffalo for a *Monday Night Football* matchup against the Bills, Jones was discussing with a visitor the team's progress and Romo's play over the first month of the season and in the Rams game in particular. "He's perfect for us," said Jones, praising the team's quarterback effusively. "His style...his heritage...his quick release and mobility...he's perfect. When he sees it, he can quickly throw. And he buys time to see it using that quick release. Once he decides to throw, he can quickly make it happen. That extra split second often gets a receiver open. He has the tools all right."

Another reason for Jones's patience was the NFL's tag rule, which allows teams to protect a key player whose contract has expired by forcing teams to pay over the next several years equivalent salaries for corresponding top players in the league. As a result, Jones was not worried about losing Romo; the quarterback could have finished the season with no new contract in hand and Jones would simply have used the franchise tag to keep him a Cowboy.

"[The tag] allows us to have [Romo] this season, next season, and the next season," said Jones. "What his agent is asking for is what I would pay if we franchise him anyway, so why would I not wait just a little bit longer and see? I will pay. Aikman was one of the top-paid quarterbacks in the game. I told [Romo's agent], 'I want him to succeed more than you do.' I need a winner. But I want to wait and see.

"I'm just being particular," continued Jones. "I want to make sure that every aspect is precision. This is a long-term investment and it needs to be perfect. I'm trying to be loose, watch and make sure. I am not the least bit nervous. The more I can see, the better it will be for the Cowboys. The time will come and I want to be sure and have seen everything."

Jones was not exactly playing with fire while waiting to re-sign the quarterback. He knew all along he was not letting Romo go anywhere. "If he walked in and said, 'I'm unhappy,' I would say, 'Let's sit down and fix this now.' After almost 20 years in the NFL, nobody knows as I do how hard it is to win. We have never done it when we did not have good quarterback play."

Romo did not seem to mind the wait. He was the starting quarterback for the Dallas Cowboys, earning $1.5 million per year and dating pop music star Jessica Simpson. Said Romo, "My friends who are making $40,000 a year just can't comprehend that amount of money. Obviously as I've been part of the league a little longer you start to realize that's part of the process, but I don't know what to do with more than $2 million to $3 million really."

Jones knew his quarterback was going to get the big money eventually, but he wanted to watch Romo in a pressure game on the road, and that opportunity presented itself in two days against Buffalo. He had watched Romo in practice for four years and knew the quarterback had a tendency in his younger years to force balls where they did not fit. Among the league leaders in passing efficiency, yards passing, and touchdowns thrown through the first several games, Romo was showing signs of on-field maturity early in his first season as the opening-day starter. And yes, the Cowboys were off to an undefeated start. But Jones felt a blowup might be just around the corner and he wanted to gauge the quarterback's reaction.

"Remember," Jones said, "it is still not impossible for him to fail. Not impossible at all. He can have that game any minute and I want to see how he handles it."

With those words, Jones rose from his chair, placing his jacket across the arm, and took a position in the center of the room. He remembered the first exhibition game Romo played in his second year on the team. "His first time to go in the game," he said, drawing back his arm, illustrating the move, "he pitches a knuckle ball. You rolled your eyes and said, 'So much for him. Bring in [backup quarterback Drew] Henson.' It did not look like he would ever get in the mode. You could see the talent, but he needed the maturity. The professional game is so much faster than the college game."

"We could not even waste a preseason game [starting] him at quarterback," said Jones of Romo's first two seasons. "Seemed like forever. We loved his style. Everybody knew he could wing it, but quarterbacks are a lot like jet pilots. They have to have a plan to go in, drop the bomb, and get out."

Two days after Jones reminded everyone his young quarterback was still unproven, his words proved prophetic as Romo played on the road against Buffalo. With millions watching on *Monday Night Football*, Romo had fits against Buffalo's scrambled coverages. In the first half alone, the quarterback had four interceptions and a fumble. Instead of dumping the ball to his running backs and tight end in the tight secondary coverage, Romo forced the ball harder downfield with each miscue. He did not take the easy routes underneath. Instead, Romo kept trying to get it all back at once.

Receiver Terrell Owens was visibly disgusted on the sideline, and other teammates were shaking their heads as well. Jones just watched stoically from a stadium suite, wondering what the outcome would be.

In the second half, Romo threw yet another interception and Dallas appeared headed for its first loss of the season. Two of his picks were returned for touchdowns. Cowboys backup quarterback Brad Johnson put on a helmet on the sideline, and it appeared Romo might be done. TV cameras showed Stephen Jones in a suite watching the game. His arms were crossed and his faced showed consternation. But something magical happened as the clock wound down: Romo never totally lost his confidence or poise, and led the team to a last-second comeback victory in one of the season's most dramatic finishes.

After Romo orchestrated two late scoring drives, setting up Nick Folk's 53-yard field goal with no time left to give the Cowboys a 25-24 win on the road, the result was a most improbable victory. The Cowboys scored nine points in the game's final 20 seconds, and in that brief period Romo completely overshadowed his play from the previous three quarters. Romo became the first player in the history of *Monday Night Football* to throw five interceptions and win, ultimately showing Jones exactly what he had been looking for. When Dallas had an open week in late October, the team was positioned atop the NFC East at 6-1 and Jones had seen enough. He immediately went to work with Romo's agent to get the player's new and vastly improved contract completed. The result was a six-year deal that, including bonuses and special clauses, reached $67.5 million.

"Jason Garrett and Wade Wilson have been miraculous for him," Jones said. "You ought to hear Jason Garrett talking to Romo...talking about, 'Don't drop a pass in if the linebackers are here,' or, 'Don't try to force it if the safety is there.' It's like we hired the greatest qualified tutor. Wade is the same way with him. We have the perfect coaches [for Romo]."

Midway through the regular season, everything was coming up roses for Dallas. Terrell Owens was heading toward another All-Pro season. Tonly Romo was having a breakout year. Nobody was calling Owens a distraction; on the contrary, everybody was talking about his focus and concentration. Dallas's vaunted offensive line was opening holes and protecting the quarterback, and the defense was showing signs of marked improvement, although that came in periodic waves.

In almost every way, the Dallas Cowboys had the markings of a team of destiny. The talented team was playing together, making all the right moves and getting all the right bounces.

Other than a humbling 48–27 defeat at Texas Stadium to New England, Dallas's first loss of the season, the team was all but unstoppable through the middle portion of its schedule. Almost everybody paying attention to the NFL was talking about Dallas and quarterback Tony Romo. The team showed few weaknesses until an unseasonably warm November day when the 8–1 Cowboys were hosting their NFC East rival, the Washington Redskins. Coming off a 31–20 road win at New York that gave the Cowboys a regular-season sweep of the Giants, all signs pointed to victory, considering the Redskins were injury-plagued and struggling and Dallas was playing the first of three games in a 12-day span at home. But as is usually the case when the Cowboys and Redskins meet, records and trends can often be thrown out the window.

Receiver Terrell Owens had his best game of the year, catching eight passes for 173 yards and four touchdowns, but the Cowboys had trouble putting the Redskins away. Center Andre Gurode sailed three snaps over Romo's head, and the Cowboys defense struggled against Washington's smash-mouth style. Team owner Jerry Jones watched the first half with his sons from his small end zone suite, but by the second half the pressurized contest drew him toward the field like a magnet. Walking nervously along the sideline, near head coach Wade Phillips, was Jones.

"Some of the players on this team were watching me when they were five years old!" Jones said. "They've been watching for 20 years. It is a consistency of the franchise.... You just don't often get that in sports. It's the one way to create a common thread; giving the franchise a consistent familiar face."

When Redskins linebacker Rocky McIntosh intercepted a Romo pass in the third quarter, returning it to the Dallas 3 and apparently taking all the momentum from the Cowboys, Jones stood still with a furrowed brow and clenched fists. He knows his team cannot win them all, but this was not a game to lose. Not at home. Not to the Redskins! When Texas Stadium video boards showed the interception might be in question, Jones stood close by Phillips as the coach reached for his red challenge flag, throwing it on the field. Eventually, the official confirmed the ruling on the field was overturned. The defender did not have possession of the ball. Clenched fists now pumping in the air, Jones exclaimed an exhaling, "Yes!" The Cowboys hung on to win 28–23.

After the game, Jones said he did not know what to do in the heat of the battle, pressure on his team building as the game became increasingly tense and close, so instead of retreating, he marched forward, to the field of battle. Whether his presence inspired the team to victory nobody can know for sure, but something happened in the second half that turned the team's intensity up a notch or three. The team showed mettle it had not shown in years, and folks around Dallas—Jerry Jones included—began to feel like their beloved Cowboys were back.

Undoubtedly, they were. Teams can win in one week in the NFL by fluke, but they rarely win week after week without being clearly better than their opponents. With its added offensive line depth thanks to off-season acquisitions, the mobility of Romo, the superlative, tempered play of Owens, and the even-keel, experienced temperament of Wade Phillips, the Cowboys had developed personality and the aura of a winner as the season hit the homestretch.

"Wade will handle winning well," said Jones. "He is simple in that he works with what he has. If you can blitz but are not a cover guy, he'll help you understand how you can help the team blitzing and he'll get somebody else who's better at coverage to do that job. He takes the best qualities. He does not piss people off. He talks about what you do well...and it's a good fit for this team."

Just as Leonard Davis was a good fit and just as Jason Garrett was a good fit. It was Garrett, after all, who, after the first time he got a good look at Owens, told Jones the receiver was bigger and better than he had known. Calling Owens by name would not be a problem, nor would be featuring him prominently in the offense.

"My style is to take risks," said Jones. "If you look at those decisions, each had its risks. Candidly, we're a much different team than we were last year. And a lot of it has to do with some of those decisions."

Fight for What You Believe

Journalists who cover the Cowboys on a regular basis universally value Jerry Jones's long-winded press conferences. If you cannot get a good column out of 45 minutes of straight talk from the Cowboys owner and general manager, then you have a serious professional problem. Two days before the 10-1 Cowboys hosted 10-1 Green Bay in a key, late-season NFC matchup, Jones held proverbial court much as he did for the opening of training camp, delivering juicy morsels as fast as anyone could write them down. The subject, oddly enough, had very little to do with the actual game at hand and everything to do with consumer supply and demand.

That's the thing about Jones. Scoring touchdowns for the team in his world occurs in more ways than most people could ever conceive. A Tony Romo to Jason Witten pass is one way the Cowboys can score. Another is defeating stubborn cable television companies that refuse to place the NFL Network alongside ESPN or CNN on the basic subscriber plan. So as the Cowboys prepared to face the Packers, Jones made television and access a primary subject of the pregame story line, tackling the subject head-on with a passionate fervor most observers could hardly digest.

The problem, of course, is that the fledgling NFL Network, which broadcasts certain games in the latter part of the season primarily on Thursday and Saturday nights, was not put on the expanded basic cable plan in 2007 by several of America's largest cable companies, including Comcast and Time Warner. Showing NFL games does not come cheap, and adding the NFL Network to programming would cost individual subscribers more than $1 per month. So Comcast and Time Warner offer it, but subscribers have to purchase it as part of a premium package.

"Not all our customers are passionate sports fans," said Steve Burke, Comcast's chief operating officer. "And many of them are not interested in paying more."

Incidentally, Steve Burke is the son of Dan Burke, the former head of ABC whom Jerry Jones went to see for television network advice before buying the Cowboys. Jones laughs when asked about the comparison, understanding full well the irony. But on this issue, he is not giving an inch, believing Steve Burke and Comcast and Time Warner to be in the wrong. Some broadcast systems, such as satellite operator DirecTV, embraced the NFL Network. But Jones and the NFL believed the league's proprietary network, with 24/7 football programming, to be as valuable as any leading sports networks, and were incensed over the snub by the larger cable companies. Jones's point, for professional football fans at least, carried much weight in the days before the Cowboys hosted the Packers, considering it was one of the biggest regular-season games of the year.

Scheduled exactly one week after Thanksgiving between two of the NFL's most-watched teams, the game was a coveted view, yet most of America could not watch it because their cable company did not include the NFL Network as a standard channel. Of the more than 111 million homes in the United States with televisions, only 35 million had access to the game between the two first-place NFC teams. Jones, of course, saw television value in the NFL before many owners did, so it was no coincidence that amidst the controversy Jones is chairman of the league's network committee. The NFL may have sued him a decade before for being an instigator, but most things do come full circle. In late 2007, Jones was not only a spokesperson for the NFL but also a torch-bearer for its cause.

"Millions may not see the game unless they switch to satellite," said Jones, speaking during a 45-minute press conference. "I do want to really encourage all Green Bay fans and Cowboy fans to make the switch and get off the Time Warners and Comcasts...and be able to see the ballgame."

The late-season scheduling on the network between the most-watched teams in football was no accident, Jones said, though nobody could have foreseen each team being 10-1. The NFL wants to build its network so that one day it will show college and professional games the same way ESPN does, but, unlike the venerable sports channel, the focus will be totally on football, nothing else. Ultimately, Jones said, the struggle between the network and the cable companies is "about dollars."

"Almost all my life," Jones said, "I have not sat around and said, 'Oh boy, here is a way to make a dollar.' I have always started from the fact that here is something people would be interested in, and usually if that is right and you do a good job there and get as many people as you can interested in it, the finances follow."

Dozens of journalists filling the media room at Dallas's Valley Ranch headquarters scrambled to get the notes down as fast as they could. They could envision the natural headline as they wrote: "NFL Owner Takes On American Cable Giants." Jones the showman sensed the seriousness, throwing them a less-serious bone.

"But what really I want to talk about," he said, "is our game plan and what we'll be running [against Green Bay], but I don't have that in my mind yet."

The room broke up in laughter.

Fortunately for Jones, the Cowboys cruised against the Packers with a convincing 37–27 victory, delighting fans who made the game's ticket one of the hottest in Dallas regular-season history. The team was suddenly the one to beat in the NFC, but the challenge would only grow tougher with three out of the final four games on the road. When the Cowboys played at Detroit the following week, they looked nothing like the team that thumped one opponent after another in the early and middle portions of the season.

The Lions ran the ball at will and, using a blitzing defensive scheme similar to the one that confounded Romo in Buffalo, threw the Cowboys offense off its rhythm. Detroit rushed for 152 yards while Dallas rushed for just 87, and the Lions controlled the ball longer and had more total yards. Yet Romo managed to throw a 16-yard touch-down pass to tight end Jason Witten, leading the team to a dramatic 28–27 win, a 12–1 record, and its first NFC East championship since 1998. Speaking in his office days after the game, Jones had conflicting emotions about the result. On the one hand, he was thrilled with the poise and comeback. Romo completed more than a dozen passes to running backs and tight ends, finding outlets from the Lions' pressure. On the other hand, he was concerned about the team's sagging play and its ability to make a run through the end of the season and the upcoming playoffs.

"Detroit," he said, "just gutted us. I knew we had not practiced enough [against the run]. We were not ready, but we made the adjustments later in the game and got it done. On offense, we did the same thing; we adjusted. Detroit was doing the same things Buffalo did early in the year.

"But let me tell you what," Jones continued. "It was the most impressed I have been with Tony Romo. He has come full circle. I said after the game, 'Fellas, we have ourselves a quarterback.' He's just evolved so much mentally...to be able to throw 12 to 15 times to the tight end and 10 to 12 times to a running back? I said, 'Boy, is he getting it now!'"

The problem with reaching a pinnacle is that staying there becomes even harder. One week in the NFL can change everything, and for the Dallas Cowboys, it did. Because the team had experienced late-season slides in recent years—losing two of the final three regular-season games in 2003, 2004, 2005, and 2006—all eyes were on the Texas team as Christmas neared.

"That has been our identity, unfortunately," Cowboys linebacker Bradie James admitted. "We need to change that identity."

Know When to Reload

When fortune is in favor of a talented and well-coached football team, winning can look easy. But when fate on the football field turns, often there is very little any coach, owner, or player can do about it. Dallas reached its pinnacle too soon in 2007 and the last-second, headlines-making victory at Detroit would be the team's last moment of celebration. When the Philadelphia Eagles visited Texas Stadium on December 16, delivering a 10-6 defeat to Dallas while Romo's new girlfriend, Jessica Simpson, watched from the stands, Dallas fans began to say, "Uh-oh, here comes trouble."

Romo was on his way to shattering franchise records for touchdown passes (36) and passing yards (4,211) on the season, yet he was dreadful against the Eagles, battling a bruised thumb he received in the third quarter. He passed for just 214 yards against the Eagles in the home loss while the month before, on the road, he had thrown for three touchdowns and 324 yards in a convincing 38–17 win. After losing to the Eagles, Romo found his honeymoon as a starting quarterback was over.

"Worry about the game," a woman yelled to Romo after the game in the Texas Stadium parking lot as he lifted the tailgate of his SUV, "not your girlfriend."

The pressurized tone would follow Dallas throughout the rest of the season, for with winning comes scrutiny. The Cowboys traveled to Washington two weeks later, with NFC home-field advantage for the playoffs firmly clinched, and rushed for a solitary yard in a 27–6 thrashing that ended the regular season. With a first-round playoff bye and the New York Giants coming to town for the divisional round playoff game, the Cowboys tried to regroup, but it was not easy. The primary story leading up to the game was whether Jerry Jones was going to fire Wade Phillips if the team lost. The Cowboys had just won the team's first division title in almost a decade and the coach's future was in question before the first playoff game kicked off.

Three days before the Giants game, Jones answered the questions patiently and politely, holding another 45-minute press conference in which he covered every topic from the team's customary late-season slide to the future of Phillips. Nothing, he said, can happen in the playoffs that would change his thinking about Phillips being the head coach of the Dallas Cowboys.

Behind the scenes Jones was a bit more frustrated with the topic being such an issue after the team won 13 regular-season games. Only once in his tenure as owner and general manager had a Dallas head coach not gotten at least *three seasons* to try to win a playoff game, and Chan Gailey, who lasted two, never won more than nine games in a year.

"There really should be no question here," he said. "It's only been 10 months [since Phillips was hired]."

Conventional wisdom among many media members covering the Cowboys, though, was that Jones did not want to lose Jason Garrett, the team's offensive coordinator, who was already under serious consideration for open NFL head coaching jobs. Jones knew the Cowboys were going to lose some coaches, all right. That is what happens when a team has success during the regular season. All indications were that new Miami director of operations Bill Parcells would hire Dallas offensive line coach Tony Sparano to coach the Dolphins. He could not hold onto everyone, but Jones had no intention of letting Garrett get away, just as he had no intention of firing Phillips.

With more than 30 years in the league, Phillips had only a few years remaining, but Jones, as the media rightly suspected, gets along with Garrett as well as any coach he has ever worked with. Garrett is young and Jones wants him on the Cowboys sideline into the future.

"There was never a question about his [Garrett's] people skills," said Jones. "When you leave the room, it [the decision] was your idea. But you know he had it all along before you got to it. This decision [hiring Garrett as offensive coordinator despite his lack of play-calling experience] worked out. Sometimes they bite my butt."

Even with the team's late-season slide and controversy surrounding the coaching staff's future, Jones was convinced the Cowboys would deliver under the spotlight in the NFC divisional round playoff game against the Giants. He knew the game would be close and physical, but instinct told him all the right pieces were in place. The game was also at home, where Dallas has had a decided advantage over the years.

The pregame storyline could not have been written more effectively. Romo was taking heat from fans and the media for taking a trip with Simpson and teammate Jason Witten to the beaches of Cabo San Lucas, Mexico, during the team's break before the playoff game. Jones did not have a problem with his quarterback's vacation, nor did Phillips, though nearly everyone else seemed to.

Romo is the player who botched the chip-shot field-goal attempt hold in the waning minutes of the Cowboys' 2007 Wild Card playoff game against Seattle, resulting in a difficult-to-accept franchise loss. And Romo is the one who, after gaining Jones's trust and a huge multiyear contract extension, went on an end-of-the-year slide, throwing just one touchdown pass in the Cowboys' last three games—two of them losses.

If Romo was feeling pressure, so was Phillips, though most of it was self-imposed. His job was secure all right, but Phillips had never won a playoff game in his head coaching career, losing each of three tries in stops at Denver and Buffalo. The most memorable was the "Music City Miracle" of 2000, the game in which the Tennessee Titans scored on a questionable, last-second lateral during a kickoff return. The "Music City Mistake" is how Phillips's wife, Laurie, remembers the game, and both she and her husband wanted to shake it off with a win over the Giants.

Once the game began, everything seemed to come together for the Cowboys. Receiver Terrell Owens, questionable with a high ankle sprain, had worked his way into the lineup by pushing himself through the most rigorous rehab schedule anyone could recall. Owens rehabbed on Christmas Day. Owens rehabbed on New Year's Day. Owens rehabbed hours upon hours each and every day, working across town on the Dallas Mavericks' underwater treadmill, which allowed him to stay in shape without stressing the ankle.

From the start, Dallas's offense clicked. Coaches had made Marion Barber the starter at running back instead of Julius Jones, hoping to benefit from his more powerful style, and it worked throughout the first half as the Cowboys smashed their way to a 14-7 lead. In the end, though, it was not enough. Romo and the Cowboys played well enough, considering they held a 336 to 230 yards gained advantage. But the Cowboys had been penalty prone all season and 11 flags for 84 yards in the game hurt them.

Jones walked from his suite to his customary post on the Dallas sideline in the waning minutes of the close game, trying to cheer his team to victory, and he had every bit of confidence the better team would win. The Cowboys had the ball in their hands at the Giants' 48-yard line with 1:50 to play, trailing 21-17. It was not meant to be for Dallas, however, as Romo's desperate fourth-down pass with under a minute to play was intercepted in the end zone. In the bowels of Texas Stadium following the game, Jones said the loss was perhaps his most painful as an owner. One journalist who has covered the Cowboys for more than a decade said he had never seen Jones look so bad after a game. Almost two decades of frustrations usurped just like that.

"I'm dying," he said. "I'm absolutely dying."

Football can be a cruel game, especially to one who loves it as much as Jerry Jones does. But in defeat, he refused to let it get the best of him. Less than 48 hours after the Cowboys lost, Jones was up early on a Tuesday morning, taking a telephone call from his Highland Park home. His voice was scratchy, rough from too little sleep and too much stress, yet he didn't back down during his weekly radio show from talking about the devastating loss. Not many minutes passed, though, before Jones was talking about the future. The franchise, he says, has every reason to be optimistic. The talent level has never been better. The new stadium is well under way. Wade Phillips is a good coach and nobody plans to let Jason Garrett get away easily.

Over the next two weeks, Jones traveled to Alabama to analyze talent playing in the annual collegiate Senior Bowl, and he successfully convinced Garrett to stay by giving the assistant coach more team responsibility and a raise to $3 million in salary per year. Some assistant coaches departed, like Sparano, but positions were filled with some familiar faces, including new defensive backs coach and former Cowboys head coach Dave Campo. By the time February 2008 rolled around and those dogged New York Giants, whom the Cowboys dismantled twice during the regular season, were celebrating a Super Bowl victory, Jones was feeling better about his team than ever before. Dallas was well positioned in the 2008 NFL Draft, selelcting running back Felix Jones and cornerback Mike Jenkins in the first round, and Jones and the organization were busy planning to put the Blue Star back on top of the NFL.

Afterword

Afterword

In the nine months and change that I researched this book, the prevailing question I was asked was always the same. Nobody asked what it was like in the Cowboys locker room. Nor did they ask whether Tony Romo has big dimples or whether Terrell Owens was as colorful off the field as he seems on the field. What everybody wanted to know is what Jerry Jones is really like in person.

At first, I was thrown by the inquisition. Nobody as complex as one of the richest self-made Americans, who also happens to be owner and general manager of one of the most recognized sports franchises and brands in the world, can be described in just a few words. Eventually, however, I adapted, coming up with the best answer I could think of.

Read the book.

The question stems, I guess, from the fact that most people know Jerry Jones only through sound bites, whether he's on television, talking to a reporter, or waxing on during one of his many radio interviews. In those environments, Jones is part enthusiast, part manager, and part showman.

Consider the moment I was in Jones's office when he was doing his weekly Friday morning radio show with Norm Hitzges, the longtime Dallas sports commentator and analyst. Sitting behind his desk, Jones was the showman. In essence, he had on the same suit and tie he wore as a young man, greeting customers as they entered his family's grocery store when he was a child back in Arkansas.

When the first question from Hitzges landed about Jones's involvement in the abrupt hiring in late 2007 of Atlanta Falcons head coach

Bobby Petrino by the University of Arkansas, his alma mater and the school he contributes substantially to as an alumnus, Jones never wavered, displaying a confident answer with a touch of on-air swagger.

"That was [Petrino] driving the car all the way," he said, looking up for emphasis. "I wanted to make sure [Falcons owner] Arthur Blank and [Falcons general manager] Rich McKay knew what was going on every step of the way. I talked with them before the Monday night game [held days before Petrino quit to take the Arkansas job], and at no time have I visited with Petrino. Was I a conduit? No. My sensitivity was about [Blank's and McKay's] relationship."

When discussing whether former Dallas coach Bill Parcells deserved credit for the Cowboys' winning 2007 season more than current coach Wade Phillips, Jones gave emphatic pause, before answering with conviction. "Bill had his best year with Dave Campo's players, if you want to look at it that way," Jones said. "But that's a B.S. way to look at it. Each year is different."

And when he was asked about the dancing skills of Wade Phillips, which led to another question about former Cowboys running back Emmitt Smith and Dallas Mavericks owner Mark Cuban appearing on the popular reality TV series *Dancing With the Stars*, he gave a rather surprising answer.

"*Dancing with the Stars?*" Jones said. "No. I'm not taking the call. They've already called."

"They've already called?" asked Hitzges.

"Yes. And I said no."

On-air laughter.

With each question, Jones gave answers that were true but also worthy of a sound bite, understanding listeners tune in to be entertained. Talk-show sponsors do not want droll talk; they want a showman on the air. But after Jones hung up the telephone, sending Hitzges to the radio station's listener lines for discerning follow-up debate, the Dallas owner and general manager made a transformation. In an instant, Jones went from being a bigger-than-life sports celebrity figure to being a quieter, more humble figure. He inquired about the family of his guest as dozens of photos of children and grandchildren surrounded his desk.

Before too long, the visitor realized the conversation had moved away from the tasks and subjects at hand. Discussion turned once again to football, specifically the approaching playoffs and the challenge of reaching another Super Bowl. At midmorning on a Friday, no journalists were around. The office was quiet, except for an occasional noise made by his assistant in another room. She interrupted once to see whether Jones wanted to tape his weekly television spot. If so, they were ready for him.

No, he said. See if Stephen can do it instead.

"If he's dressed [properly] just let him," said Jones.

Conversation continued. The Cowboys were having one of the best seasons in franchise history. Expectations were running high. Publicly Jones had talked for months about everything the team had done right, about how they expected to win. But even the optimistic owner in his quieter moments knows it is not that easy.

"From years of experience," said Jones, "nobody knows better than I do how hard it is to win in this league."

Notes

Notes

Chapter 1

"If this doesn't work...": *The Dallas Morning News*, 2003; www.apse. dallasnews.com.

"Everybody thought Pat was crazy...": *The Dallas Morning News*, September 9, 2007.

"My dad once said...": *The Dallas Morning News*, September 9, 2007.

"Scared wasn't the word...": *The Dallas Morning News*, July 27, 1989.

"You are going to wake...": *The Dallas Morning News*, September 9, 2007.

"If you're so sure...": Krugel, Mitchell, *Texas Football Trilogy* (Champaign, IL: Sports Publishing, 2000).

"I've never gone to sleep...": *The Sporting News*, September 18, 1995.

Rural in nature...: *The Sporting News*, September 18, 1995.

"Now I think I'm going to die...": The Associated Press, April 19, 2007.

"The Cowboys were my...": *Sports Illustrated*, July 10, 2007.

"Tails...": *The Dallas Morning News*, February 25, 2004.

Chapter 2

"It [change] happens in every business...": *The Dallas Morning News*, February 26, 1989.

"I'm here and Jimmy's here...": *The Dallas Morning News*, February 26, 1989.

"I've been scared for the last...": *The Dallas Morning News*, April 19, 1989.

"It's great to be a Cowboy...": *The Dallas Morning News*, April 19, 1989.

"That does not mean...": *USA Today*, March 21, 1989.

Chapter 3
"I don't sit around here and worry…": *Fort Worth Star-Telegram*, September 24, 1989.
"But you've got a way…": *The Dallas Morning News*, September 2, 1989.
"This new ownership…": *Fort Worth Star-Telegram*, September 28, 1989.
"Last-place Cowboys…": *Dallas Times Herald*, November 20, 1989.
"The longer you criticize…": *Dallas Times Herald*, April 26, 1991.
"Look," Bayless said…: *Dallas Times Herald*, August 6, 1989.
"You'll do all right…": *Forbes*, February 19, 1990.
"He [Jones] can sell…": *Dallas Times Herald*, March 2, 1991.
"Who is running the football…": *Texas Monthly*, June 1994.
"If Bob came to me…": *Fort Worth Star-Telegram*, May 23, 1992.

Chapter 4
"We have operated in a fearless…": *The Kansas City Star*, October 16, 1992.
"This is what the job…": *Fort Worth Star-Telegram*, September 3, 1992.
"I want Jerry…": *Fort Worth Star-Telegram*, September 3, 1992.
"Where I sit, I cannot…": *The Dallas Morning News*, January 15, 1993.
"I paid a great deal…": *The Washington Post*, January 29, 1993.
"In all candor…": *The Dallas Morning News*, January 11, 1993.
When sitting for…: *The Washington Post*, January 29, 1993.
"Our communication…": *Fort Worth Star-Telegram*, January 27, 1993.
"I thought, How could…": *American Way* magazine, January 1, 2008.

Chapter 5
"We've had issues…": *Dallas Times Herald*, August 2, 1991.
"I should have fired him…": *The Dallas Morning News*, March 23, 1994.
"I've heard from numerous reliable sources…": *The Dallas Morning News*, March 23, 1994.
The right thing…: *The Dallas Morning News*, January 15, 1996.
"It worked so great for us…": ESPN.com, November 23, 1999.

Switzer remembers Jones as a "try hard guy...": *Texas Monthly*, June 1994.

Consider the story of Jones...: *Texas Monthly*, June 1994.

He blasted Jones and Switzer...: *Fort Worth Star-Telegram*, April 5, 1994.

"The NFL looking into something...": *The Dallas Morning News*, November 16, 1994.

Chapter 6

"I know that this son...": *The Sporting News*, March 13, 1995.

"Cowboys owner bucks...": *The New York Times*, September 24, 1995.

"The league will die...": *San Jose Mercury News*, August 23, 1995.

"The man's gone too far...": *Sports Illustrated*, October 18, 1995.

"He's going to tear...": *Sports Illustrated*, October 18, 1995.

The league sought damages...: *The New York Times*, September 24, 1995.

According to biographer Carlo DeVito...:DeVito, Carlo, *Wellington: The Maras, the Giants, and the City of New York*; (Chicago, IL: Triumph Books, 2006).

"Score another victory...": *The Business Journal* (Milwaukee), December 20, 1996.

"Money is how...": *The Sporting News*, March 13, 1995.

"Even my father at the end...": *New York Daily News*, November 21, 2007.

"We did it!": *The Sporting News*, February 5, 1996.

"I just want to say...": The Associated Press, January 26, 1996.

"If anyone is willing...": *The Washington Post*, January 29, 1993.

Chapter 7

"It's a very hard...": *The Dallas Morning News*, September 29, 2003.

"We won't be as...": *The Sporting News*, January 28, 1996.

"We'd like to think...": *The Sporting News*, January 28, 1996.

"To get better at something...": *Amarillo Globe*, July 28, 1998.

"But he [Jones] did the right thing...": *The Sporting News*, January 28, 1996.

"There are just too many...": *The New York Times*, September 21, 1997.

"I understand it's my...": The Associated Press, January 12, 2000.

"Jerry has the sense to step up...": Krugel, Mitchell, *Texas Football Trilogy* (Champaign, IL: Sports Publishing, 2000).

"It's understandable to have...": *The New York Times*, September 29, 2003.

"That was a stupid...": *The Dallas Morning News*, December 9, 2002.

Chapter 8

"Is he [Jones] striving...": *The Sporting News*, January 28, 1996.

"I could work...": *The New York Times*, September 29, 2003.

"It would be recognition...": *The New York Times*, September 29, 2003.

"You hit some home runs...": *The New York Times*, September 29, 2003.

"We have had 30 years...": www.athleticbusiness.com, March 1, 2005.

Residents had rejected...: ESPN.com, October 31, 2004.

"This campaign is about...": ESPN.com, October 31, 2004.

"If you extend that...": *American Way* magazine, January 2008.

"It [the Astrodome] just sucked the air...": *Sports Illustrated*, July 10, 2007.

"It really gave me some...": *American Way* magazine, January 2008.

"You did not know what...": *Sports Illustrated*, July 21, 2007.

Chapter 9

"I think you have risk...": www.dallascowboys.com, March 18, 2006.

"Any time you do...": The Associated Press, October 25, 2006.

Bill Parcells's Quarterback Commandments: ESPN, October 8, 2007.

The Cowboys on the other hand...: *Dallas Observer*, March 16, 2006.

"They take more frequent and...": *Dallas Observer*, March 16, 2006.

"We take it all with...": *Dallas Observer*, March 16, 2006.

When Wade Phillips met...: *The Dallas Morning News*, February 9, 2007.

"We needed to get it right...": The Associated Press, February 9, 2007.

"I think he [Jones]...": *Forbes*, March 2007.

"Would you...": *The Dallas Morning News*, May 17, 2007.

"I can count on one...": *Sports Illustrated*, July 10, 2007.

"When you've won...": *The New York Times*, September 29, 2003.

Chapter 10

On the day at hand...: *The Dallas Morning News*, September 9, 2007.

"I was hugging him...": *The Dallas Morning News*, October 1, 2007.

"Don't give up...": *The Dallas Morning News*, October 1, 2007.

"Not all our customers...": *The Wall Street Journal*, August 26, 2007.

"That has been our identity...": *Fort Worth Star-Telegram*, November 24, 2007.

"Worry about the game...": *The Dallas Morning News*, December 17, 2007.

"I'm dying...": *The Dallas Morning News*, January 15, 2008.